Understanding and Using COFF

Understanding and Using COFF

O'Reilly & Associates, Inc.
632 Petaluma Avenue
Sebastopol, CA 95472

Understanding and Using COFF
by Gintaras R. Gircys

Editor: Tim O'Reilly

Printing History:

November 1988:   First Edition.

ISBN: 0-937175-31-5   [8/93]

TABLE OF CONTENTS

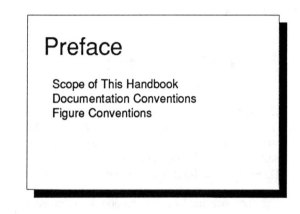

Preface

Scope of This Handbook
Documentation Conventions
Figure Conventions

COFF—Common Object File Format—is the formal definition for the structure of machine code files in the UNIX System V environment. All machine code files, whether fully linked executables, compiled applications, or system libraries, are COFF structure files.

Knowledge of COFF is becoming increasingly important as the UNIX operating system gains in popularity. There is hardly a system related task that does not require some knowledge of COFF. COFF knowledge is also vital to the growing number of software engineers that develop cross applications and special proprietary enhancements to the UNIX operating system.

Lastly, knowledge of COFF is an absolute requirement for entry into the realm of the truly sophisticated UNIX elite. The COFF system is intrinsic to some of the most interesting areas of the kernel such as the loader, and COFF concepts directly affect the design of efficient memory swapping/paging mechanisms. COFF is also in the forefront of exciting new developments in the UNIX operating system such as shared libraries and the new proposed "Applications Binary Interface" from Sun and AT&T.

Whether your need for understanding COFF is task driven, or simply healthy curiosity, this handbook will teach you the basics of COFF, and expand your knowledge of the UNIX operating system not only with particular details, but more importantly, with the powerful philosophical concepts behind COFF that make UNIX a portable and extensible operating system.

Scope of This Handbook

This handbook teaches you all of the essential details and intentions of AT&T's UNIX System V COFF definition. Much of the conceptual information presented in this handbook also applies to the Berkeley Software Distribution (BSD) UNIX operating system environment. That is because BSD *a.out* format is COFF's ancestor.

The approach used by this handbook in describing COFF is generic—it does not describe any particular implementation. This is in keeping with the true spirit of COFF. However, once the concepts of this handbook are mastered, you can quickly and efficiently integrate the machine/implementation dependent information particular to your UNIX operating system environment with the generic concepts presented in this handbook.

Chapter 1   explains what COFF is and where it is used within the UNIX system. The creation and use of COFF files is explained along with the major utilities that manipulate COFF files. Lastly, this chapter explains the conceptual philosophy behind the COFF definition, its benefits, and introduces the major components of the COFF file.

Chapter 2   describes how UNIX assemblers implement relocatable code. The explanation details how machine code is manipulated and explains the use of pertinent assembler directives such as .text, .data, and .bss.

Chapter 3 covers the information found in the COFF file headers. The headers include magic numbers, run-time information, and more. This chapter explains the contents and uses of the headers, and includes a section that explains the general use of COFF-structure file pointers to access areas of the COFF file.

Chapter 4 introduces the basics of the relocation process. This includes a description of the three COFF structures used in the relocation process: section headers, relocation entries, and symbol table entries, and how they are used by the linker to perform relocation. Linker pseudo-algorithms are used to explain a trivial link.

Chapter 5 expands on the previous chapter by explaining the relocation process for a realistic scenario where several files with symbolic dependencies are linked. Relocation within a data section is also explained.

Chapter 6 introduces several important places within UNIX where COFF is used. This includes an explanation of how the kernel loader and linker use COFF section-type information, how COFF supports common data, and how to use partial linking. This chapter also includes a detailed explanation about archive files—their format and special linker interface, and how they are manipulated by the *ar* utility.

Chapter 7 is all about magic. Magic numbers that is. The byte flip-flop problem and how it pertains to magic numbers is also explained.

Chapter 8 is all about the COFF symbolic debug system. This chapter is of special interest to compiler and assembler writers, assembly language programmers, and debug system programmers. This lengthy chapter covers all aspects of the COFF symbolic debug system: symbol table entries and use, line numbers, special assembler directives, string table structure, symbol table format, and more. The chapter ends with a discussion on extending the COFF symbolic system to accommodate other languages.

Chapter 9   demonstrates how a major enhancement, shared libraries, is folded into the COFF definition. The explanation introduces the major concepts and components of the shared library system such as host and target libraries, special .init and .lib sections, and the *mkshlib* utility.

Chapter 10   lists a number of useful utilities for working with COFF files. A brief explanation of each utility is provided. The chapter also provides some helpful hints on using header files and introduces the COFF special-function library, *libld.a*.

Chapter 11   presents a comprehensive C source-code program for working with COFF files. The program can serve as the foundation for any COFF file project—from a utility that dumps raw data to a PROM programmer, to a sophisticated object file editor. Access to every area of the COFF file is demonstrated.

Appendix A   contains a quick reference and summary of the most important and often encountered COFF structures and their related mnemonics.

Documentation Conventions

This handbook uses **bold** and *italicized* text to emphasize special words.

Bold   is used for words and phrases that you should pay special attention to. These words could be the names of system utilities, assembler directives, or any word that is central to the topic under discussion.

Italics   are used to represent generic terms that require context-dependent substitution. For example, *integer* means to use some appropriate numerical value. Italics are also used to refer to UNIX filenames, directories, and commands.

`Constant Width`	font is used for sample code fragments and examples. A reference in explanatory text to a word or item used in an example or code fragment is also shown in constant width font.
function(n)	is a reference to a man page section *n* describing *function*. All man page references in this handbook are references to either the *System V User's Reference Manual* (Section 1), or the *System V Programmer's Reference Manual* (Section 3).
numbers	in assembly-listing examples (addresses and machine instruction coding values) are hexadecimal. Otherwise, numeric representation in general follows the standard UNIX convention where hex values are in the form 0x*nnnn*; octal values are in the form 0*nnnn*; and decimal numbers are simply *nnnn*. Whenever necessary, the base of the number is explicitly stated.

Figure Conventions

This handbook contains a number of figures that diagram the many relationships between the various COFF structures. To help you get the most out of these figures, three special conventions are used when diagraming structural relationships. The convention used depends on how the structure's particular field value is interpreted. In general, a field's value can have one of the following three interpretations:

- The field can contain a **file-offset value**. This value can be used directly as an argument to the `fseek` function in order to position for reading a specific area of the COFF file. An example of this type of field is the `f_symptr` field in the `filehdr` structure. `f_symptr` is a file-offset value that points to the start of the symbol table.

- The field can contain a **relative-offset value**. This value most often is used in a calculation that determines a specific member or entry (similar to array indexing). An example of this type of field is the `r_symndx` field of the relocation entry structure, `reloc`. `r_symndx` is an index into the symbol table.

- The field can contain an **absolute value**. This value represents an absolute number and in the diagrams most often specifies some relevant quantity (as opposed to a flag value). An example of this field is the f_nsyms field of the filehdr structure. f_nsyms represents the number of symbol table entries.

In the diagrams, each of the three different interpretations is represented in its own special way:

- A **file-offset** is represented by a **solid line** with arrows. The arrows point to the relevant location specified by the file-offset value.

- A **relative-offset** is represented by a **dash-dot line** with arrows. The arrows point to the relevant location specified by the relative-offset value.

- An **absolute** value is represented by a **dotted line** with arrows. The arrows point to the relevant location that can use the absolute value in calculating some needed operation such as a loop sequence.

The next page gives an example of the three uses and how they are represented.

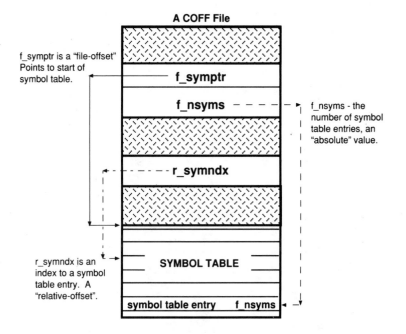

A COFF File

f_symptr is a "file-offset" Points to start of symbol table.

f_symptr

f_nsyms – – – – → f_nsyms - the number of symbol table entries, an "absolute" value.

r_symndx

r_symndx is an index to a symbol table entry. A "relative-offset".

SYMBOL TABLE

symbol table entry   f_nsyms

This diagram illustrates how the relationships of the three different types of field value uses are represented in the COFF road map diagrams.

Solid lines with arrows are used for "file-offset" values. The arrows point to the area referenced by the file-offset value.

Dash-dot lines with arrows are used for "relative-offset" values. The arrows point to the area referenced by the relative-offset value.

Dotted lines are used for absolute values. The arrows point to an area that represents the absolute value's use or meaning.

Figure 1. Figure Conventions

The Basics of COFF

The Assembly Code
Relocation Process

COFF File Headers

Relocation Structures/
Relocation Process

The Linking Process

The COFF System in UNIX

Magic Numbers

The COFF Symbolic
Debug System

COFF and Shared Libraries

Utilities and Techniques for
Working with COFF Files

A Sample COFF Program

1

The Basics of COFF

What Is COFF?
Some Places Where COFF Is Used
Where Do COFF Files Come From?
Where Do COFF Files Go?
The Basic Element of the COFF Definition
Benefits of COFF

This chapter introduces the basics of COFF.

The chapter begins at a pretty basic level for good reason. COFF jargon is used with reckless abandon in much of the existing COFF-related documentation. If you are fairly new to the UNIX environment, a sound and consistent definition of terms makes the learning experience much easier, and leaves you with a clear conceptual picture of what COFF is, and where COFF fits in.

Once the terminology and hierarchy issues are finished, this chapter proceeds to introduce the details of the COFF structure.

1

What Is COFF?

COFF—Common Object File Format—is the formal definition for the structure of all UNIX System V machine code files. For instance, every machine code executable file (as opposed to an executable shell script) is a COFF structure file. Object files, the output from either compilers or assemblers, also are COFF files. Archived libraries, like *libc.a*, are nothing more than collections of COFF object files. COFF files are to the UNIX operating system what atoms are to matter.

The COFF definition describes a complex data structure that represents object files, executable files, and archive files. The COFF data structure defines fields for machine code, relocation information, symbolic information, and more. The contents of these fields are accessed by an organized system of pointers. UNIX assemblers, compilers, linkers, debuggers, and archivers (just to name a few) manipulate the contents of the COFF data structure to achieve their particular objective.

This handbook explains the details of COFF data structure and its manipulation. Understanding these details is valuable information that is relevant to many UNIX systems programming task—from understanding assembly source to implementing a proprietary system enhancement.

Some Places Where COFF Is Used

Many areas within UNIX are affected by the COFF definition. For example, the object files created by UNIX assemblers are usually **relocatable**. This means that the machine code is not restricted to a specific memory range. The linker uses **relocation** information in the COFF object file to patch the relevant areas of machine code with the proper run-time address. The linker also sets a special **magic number** if a file is executable. The magic number is used by the system to determine whether the file is executable or not. The COFF definition includes information that presents the state (executable or not, debug information present or stripped, etc.) of the COFF file to the system.

UNIX compilers also use the COFF definition. The COFF definition includes comprehensive information on source code symbolics. This allows the implementation of powerful symbolic debuggers such as *sdb*. Compiler-created symbolic information is used by *sdb* to implement high-level debug features such as tracing a program's execution in the source, and symbolic access to program variables. The COFF definition includes information that makes these features possible.

The UNIX archive utility, *ar*, creates library files. Library files are collections of COFF object files that are organized in a special way that greatly improves the efficiency of the linking process. The *ar* utility makes use of the COFF definition to implement the efficient organization of library files.

Major enhancements to the UNIX system often involve the COFF definition. For example, **shared libraries** in UNIX System V.3 implement a technique where only one copy of a library (like *libc.a*) needs to be resident in memory even though many processes are using its functions. This results in smaller executable files and improved system performance. The COFF definition plays a major role in integrating this enhancement into UNIX.

Figure 1-1 shows the various utilities that operate on COFF files—from creation to application.

Where Do COFF Files Come From?

UNIX high-level language compilers (such as the C compiler) rarely, if ever, produce machine code as their output. Instead, UNIX compilers produce assembly-source text files and then automatically invoke the assembler. These assembly-source text files typically are named *filename.s* (**s** for assembler source) where the *filename* portion is the same as the name of the compiler source file. The assembly source text file is used as input to the assembler, and it's the assembler that finally converts human readable text into machine code and program data. The assembler's output file is a COFF file, typically named *filename.o* (**o** for object) where the *filename* portion is the same as the assembly-text source filename.

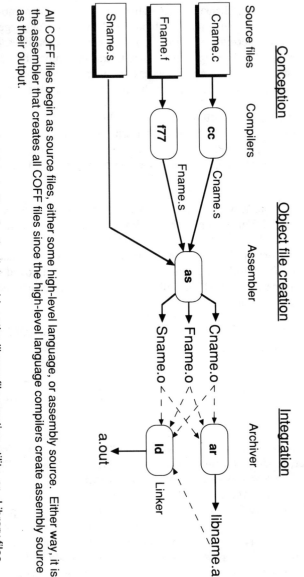

All COFF files begin as source files, either some high-level language, or assembly source. Either way, it is the assembler that creates all COFF files since the high-level language compilers create assembly source as their output.

Object files can be used as input either for the linker, ld, or the library file creation utility, ar. Library files are nothing more than handy collections of object files. The output from the linker is an executable COFF file. a.out is the default name for the linker produced executable file.

Figure 1-1.   COFF file life cycle

Though the assembler produces a COFF file that contains machine code, this file is not executable on the UNIX system. Before the file can execute, it must have the correct **magic number**; how this happens is explained shortly.

The assembler produced COFF files are usually referred to simply as **object** files; this handbook from this point on uses this term for an assembler produced, non-executable, COFF file.

Occasionally you might see the term **initial file**. This is an archaic term meaning object file. It is seldom, if ever, seen in contemporary UNIX documentation.

Where Do COFF Files Go?

There are two things you can do with an object (COFF) file. The most obvious thing is to get it to execute on the system—after all, that is the point of writing programs. This is where the linker comes into the picture.

The Linker

The UNIX linker, usually called *ld*, takes the assembler produced object file as input, does its magic on it, and produces an **executable file**. The executable file, by default, is named *a.out*, the traditional name for UNIX system executable files. Of course having more than one executable file named a.out becomes very confusing, so the usual practice is to override the default name by using the linker's output filenaming ability. The linker's output file is typically named to meaningfully represent the function that the executable file performs. The linker's output file is also a COFF file, but a COFF file with special characteristics that make it executable in the UNIX system. Executable COFF files are produced only by the linker and are typically referred to as executable files; this handbook from this point on uses this term to refer to linker produced executable files.

The UNIX linker is called *ld*, yet it is not apparent where the *d* comes from. *ld* is an acronym for **link editor**, and that's how the linker is referred to in most UNIX documentation. But this handbook refers to the link editor as the linker, for the same reason that the the link editor is invoked by the name *ld*—fewer keystrokes. UNIX commands are notorious for saving keystrokes.

The Relocation Process

The relocation process is performed by the linker on object files to turn them into executable files. The linker uses the object file's **relocation information** to create an executable file. The relocation information specifies regions in the machine code that are memory references to either data or subroutines. The addresses of these references in the object file usually do not represent the run-time address of the data or subroutines. The linker uses the relocation information to **patch** the relevant locations in the machine code of the object file with the addresses needed at run-time.

The Resolution Process

The resolution process is performed by the linker to **resolve** external symbolic references. The address of an external data or subroutine reference is unknown; therefore, the machine code in an object file requires patching by the linker. External symbolic references result in the creation of relocation information, but the actual address of the symbolic reference, its definition, resides in a different source file. The source file containing the definition, when assembled, has its own object file that must be linked with the object file containing the symbolic reference. In other words, the linker matches external symbolic **declarations** with their appropriate **definitions**. In UNIX terminology, the linker resolves symbolic references, or performs **resolution**.

The Magic Number

The magic number is set if relocation and resolution are successfully carried out by the linker. The file can now execute on the UNIX system.

Linker Parameters

Linker parameters define the characteristics of an executable file. The default link parameters (the process followed when no special request are made at invocation time) are usually hardcoded into UNIX linkers. This includes hardcoding such information as how to consolidate the sections of the input object files, and the memory range (or mapping) for the the executable file. The default process can be completely overridden by instructions in a linker directive file. If a linker directive file is used, the default process is ignored, and instead, the executable file's characteristics are determined by the instructions the linker finds in the linker directive file.

The examples in this handbook all use the default link process. In a few special cases where deviations from the default process are of interest, mention is made of the relevant parameters that can be changed by using a linker directive file.

The Archiver

The archiver is the second UNIX utility that manipulates COFF files. It takes object files as input and produces as its output a library file. The archiver is called *ar* for obvious keystroke-saving reasons. The library files created by the archiver are named *filename*.a, where *filename* indicates how the library's contents are used. And, of course, the **a** stands for archive.

Library files are nothing more than collections of object files, which have been archived together to ease the linking process. For example, the most commonly used UNIX library is *libc.a*, the C language library, and it contains over 250 object files. Imagine how messy linking would be if all 250 object filenames had to be specified whenever you wanted to link with *libc.a*. Also imagine how difficult it would be to track a particular version of the C library if it was contained in 250 individual, and possibly scattered, files. Creating an archive library solves both of these problems: when linking, only the library has to be specified, and the library is easy to track since it's all contained in one file. Just think of all the keystrokes the archiver saves!

COFF Filename Terminology

Often you'll hear UNIX system programmers talking about **dot s**, **dot o**, or **dot a** files. This is simply a way of referring to a group of assembler source files (`.s`), object files (`.o`), and archive files (`.a`) respectively. The word **dot** is a slang plural form for these files. So, instead of saying assembler source files to indicate plurality, you can say **dot s** files.

The Basic Element of the COFF Definition

Central to the COFF concept is a simple abstraction, an abstraction that identifies the most seminal, common denominators of all operating systems.

All modern multitasking/multiuser operating systems segregate program code into three basic categories: executable machine code, initialized program data, and uninitialized program data.

Executable machine code is a segregated category because today's modern operating systems employ various memory protection schemes, and machine code is protected from accidental modification. You cannot write into executable machine code in memory.

Initialized program data, on the other hand, is not write protected; it would be of little use if it was. Initialized program data represents values that the program finds when it starts to execute.

Uninitialized program data, like initialized data, is readable and writable, but since it does not represent any specific values, the only thing the operating system needs to know about it is how large the uninitialized area must be. This is a file space-saving feature. There is no need to represent non-values as anything in the file that represents the program.

COFF's Basic Structure

The COFF system **maps** the three abstract elements of a program: machine code, initialized data, and uninitialized data, to three corresponding special **sections** in the COFF file:

- The **text section**
- The **data section**
- The **bss section**

The COFF file also includes areas for relocation information and symbolic debug information. All of this information is organized as a data structure.

The COFF defined data structure includes an organized system of pointers that allow efficient access to, and manipulation of, any of the three sections, as well as the symbolic debug information and relocation information areas that contain information for use by the linker.

Figure 1-2 illustrates the important components of the COFF file.

Text sections contain executable machine code and the operating system treats it as write protected.

Data sections contain initialized program code and is readable and writable.

Bss sections basically contain information on how large the uninitialized data area is. The **bss section** is usually made a contiguous with the **data section** when the program is loaded into memory. All UNIX systems initialize the bss section to zeroes when it is created in memory. The bss acronym comes from the old IBM mainframe world that extensively used the space saving feature of the bss concept. bss means memory ''Block Started by Symbol''—a block of memory that is not initialized.

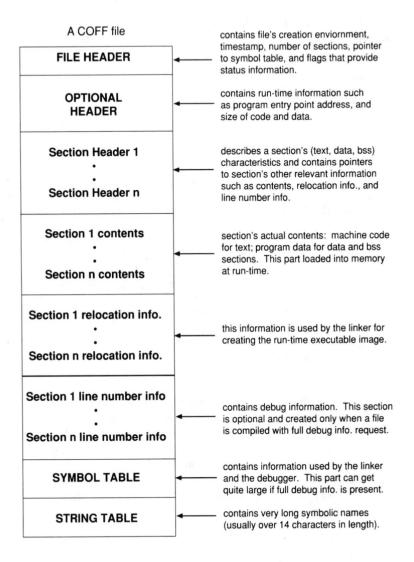

A COFF file

FILE HEADER	contains file's creation enviornment, timestamp, number of sections, pointer to symbol table, and flags that provide status information.
OPTIONAL HEADER	contains run-time information such as program entry point address, and size of code and data.
Section Header 1 • • **Section Header n**	describes a section's (text, data, bss) characteristics and contains pointers to section's other relevant information such as contents, relocation info., and line number info.
Section 1 contents • • **Section n contents**	section's actual contents: machine code for text; program data for data and bss sections. This part loaded into memory at run-time.
Section 1 relocation info. • • **Section n relocation info.**	this information is used by the linker for creating the run-time executable image.
Section 1 line number info • • **Section n line number info**	contains debug information. This section is optional and created only when a file is compiled with full debug info. request.
SYMBOL TABLE	contains information used by the linker and the debugger. This part can get quite large if full debug info. is present.
STRING TABLE	contains very long symbolic names (usually over 14 characters in length).

Figure 1-2. A COFF file's basic structure and components

Benefits of COFF

The COFF definition creates two major benefits: enhanced portability, and system extensibility.

Portability

The COFF definition enhances portability because it maps generic hardware data structures onto software data structures. Hardware-imposed data structures are not portable. Software defined data structures are more portable. Therefore, the UNIX operating system is portable because of the COFF definition.

The COFF definition makes it possible to segregate machine dependent code to a few places in the UNIX source. Most of the generic (non-device driver) UNIX operating system porting work involves only changes to the C compiler code generator, assembler, debuggers, and a few localized areas in the kernel (program entry/exit, system call service, interrupt tables, etc). Even the debugger work is not as awesome as one would think. The COFF definition includes extensive C language symbolic information that is port independent.

System Extensibility

Software defined data structures are also easily extensible. Though the **text, data** and **bss** sections are special, they are not sacrosanct. If necessary, it is possible to add sections to the COFF definition. In this case, the COFF definition provides an invaluable service as a foundation template for orderly expansion. For example, National Semiconductor's SERIES 32000 version of COFF has three sections added to it to take advantage of the 32000's modular architecture. These three new sections: static, module, and link, are very neatly folded into the COFF format, and are available to those that might want to use the SERIES 32000 modular coding technique.

The COFF definition also allows for generic extensions such as **shared libraries** or machine-independent data formats.

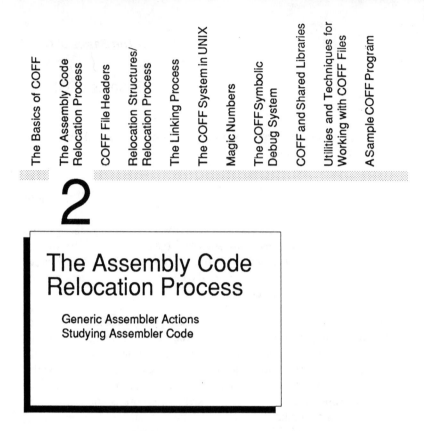

The Basics of COFF

The Assembly Code Relocation Process

COFF File Headers

Relocation Structures/ Relocation Process

The Linking Process

The COFF System in UNIX

Magic Numbers

The COFF Symbolic Debug System

COFF and Shared Libraries

Utilities and Techniques for Working with COFF Files

A Sample COFF Program

2

The Assembly Code Relocation Process

Generic Assembler Actions
Studying Assembler Code

Relocation is the technique that makes address-space-independent code (and data) possible. COFF implements relocation because treating code as address-space independent is really the only way a portable (and flexible) machine code system can be developed. The abstractions inherent in the relocation concept make it possible to segregate implementation-dependent, run-time address assignments to only one component of the program development cycle—the linker. The assembler creates relocation information since it knows what addresses need run-time assignment; the linker then uses this relocation information when it creates an executable file.

This chapter explains details of relocation with emphasis on the assembler's role in the process. If you feel comfortable with the relocation technique in general; understand the basic assembler directives such as .text, .data, .comm, and .bss; and understand the difference between defined and declared symbols, you may just skim the first few sections of this chapter to familiarize yourself with the generic assembler code examples since they are used throughout this handbook.

Generic Assembler Actions

Since assemblers work with low level machine instructions, a generic CPU is used to illustrate the COFF related relocation actions.

The generic CPU used for example code is a 32-bit machine that has only three instructions:

- add *source, destination*
- move *source, destination*
- call *destination*

The add and move instructions support two types of addressing modes:

- absolute address, represented symbolically
- register, such as r0 and r1

An absolute address is a 32-bit integer value appended to the opcode of the instruction. The call (subroutine) instruction's *destination* can be only an absolute address. (Of course there is a "ret" instruction if an example needs to show a return from a subroutine.)

This simple architecture serves tutorial needs quite well, but keep in mind that COFF has adequate implementation-dependent fields to characterize all sorts of complex architectures. For example, this simple architecture uses only absolute addressing mode, but in reality there are architectures that also use relative addressing modes, and that represent addresses in two ways—most significant byte (MSB) to least significant byte (LSB) and vice versa. This vital information can be recorded in the appropriate part of the COFF structure.

A Generic Code Example

The following commented source code example introduces the basic code structure created by the generic assembler.

```
address     opcode        source              comments
-------     ------        ------              --------

0000        01000000000c  move number, r0     # opcode = 0100
0006        02000000000c  add  number, r0     # opcode = 0200

000c        00000004      number: .double 4   # initialized data
```

When this code is executed, the value stored at number is moved into register 0, then it is added to itself with the result, 8, remaining in register 0. The important point to notice from this example is the instruction opcode coding for the symbolic reference to the symbol number. The opcodes for the move and add instructions are appended with the actual memory location of number.

In order to make this example UNIX environment realistic, UNIX assembler directives must be added. The assembler directive begin to impress the requirements of the COFF definition on the generated code.

Assembler Directives

Assembler directives are keywords for the assembler instructing it to do something special. Typically, UNIX assembler directives begin with a period (.).

Two important assembler directives implement the segregation of **text** (machine code) from **data**.

The .text Assembler Directive

The .text assembler directive tells the assembler to put the generated **machine code** in the **text section** of the output file created by the assembler.

The .data Assembler Directive

The .data assembler directive tells the assembler to put the **initialized data** in the **data section** of the output file created by the assembler.

Creating Relocation Information

Adding the .text and .data directives to the previous example makes it look like this:

```
address    opcode        source              comments
-------    ------        ------              --------
                         .text               # start text section
0000       01000000000c  move  number, r0    # opcode = 0100
0006       02000000000c  add   number, r0    # opcode = 0200

                         .data               # start data section
000c       00000004      number: .double 4   # initialized data
```

When this code is executed, the result is exactly as before. Even the instruction encoding for the symbolic access to number is exactly the same. But this is true only if two rather unreasonable assumptions are made regarding the program's execution environment in a multitasking, multiuser operating system like the UNIX operating system.

The first assumption has the program starting at memory address zero. This may not be true as the system loader may use another start address.

The second assumption has the data located contiguously with the text section, just as represented in the source listing. This is most certainly not true since hardware memory protection architectures operate on blocks of memory that are typically larger than 512 bytes. Thus, in the example, the write protection of the text section also applies to the data section. This is an undesirable situation. The data section must be in its own block of readable and writable memory, which means that the addresses appended to the add and move instructions must be greater than the contiguously derived value shown in the assembler source listing. Obviously something is missing.

Since the default addresses can't be used, the COFF system includes a category of special information called **relocation** information. The assembler creates relocation information which is subsequently used by the linker as it processes the object files created by the assembler. The output file from the link process is a file that can execute on the system. In essence, the relocation information gives the linker the areas in the machine code that have to be **patched**, or updated, to reflect the true run-time addresses.

Defined and Declared Symbols

Two words used quite often in conjunction with COFF related issues cause UNIX beginners no small amount of confusion. The words are **defined** and **declared**, and they refer to the state of symbolic references. Though at first the difference between these two words may appear semantically trivial (that's why they cause so much trouble), in reality these words describe very different and special symbolic states.

A symbol is **defined** when storage space is allocated for it.

A symbol is **declared** when its properties are announced.

The Effects of Defined and Declared Symbols

The assembler treats defined and declared symbols in a different manner. For example:

```
address    opcode            source              comments
-------    ------            ------              --------
                          .globl me         # external declaration
                          .text             # start text section
0000    030000000000    call me            # opcode = 0300
0006    02000000000c    add   number, r0   # opcode = 0200

                          .data             # start data section
000c    00000004        number: .double 4  # data definition
```

The first line of source in the example uses the assembler `.globl` directive to announce the properties of the symbol me. The symbol me is an external symbol; it resides in another source file. The effect of the `.globl` assembler directive is to declare the symbol me. The `call` instruction's reference to me results in the creation of relocation information that says that the actual address of symbol me is found in another source file. The symbol me is **explicitly** declared external by the .globl assembler directive.

The final line in the example source segment uses the assembler .double directive to allocate and initialize the symbol number to integer value 4. The symbol number is defined. The add instruction's reference to number is a **local symbolic reference**. This reference also results in the creation of relocation information, but with information that differentiates it from a relocation information for an external reference. (Note: for the remainder of this handbook, as is customary in UNIX terminology, a local symbolic reference is simply referred to as a symbolic reference.)

Many UNIX assemblers do not require an explicit external declaration. Any symbol that is referenced but not defined within the current source is automatically treated as external. For example, if the first line of source with the .globl assembler directive is omitted, the symbol me is **implicitly** declared external (as if a .globl was used). All examples in this handbook use, as good programming practice dictates, explicit external declarations. Unfortunately, in reality, good programming practices are sometimes ignored and you should, in order to avoid time wasting confusion, be on the look-out for implicit external declarations whenever examining assembler source.

Uninitialized Data

Uninitialized data sections, like text and data sections, are created by using the appropriate assembler directive. There are two commonly used assembler directives for symbolically setting aside uninitialized storage space.

The following example demonstrates the use of both directives:

```
address          source
-------          ------
0000       .bss  foo1,2,4
0002       .comm foo2,16
```

In neither case are the symbols initialized to a particular value. The fact that both appear as zero at program run-time results from how the system handles bss data.

The .bss Assembler Directive

The .bss assembler directive defines the symbol fool by setting aside two bytes of storage space that is aligned to a four byte boundary.

The .comm Assembler Directive

The .comm assembler directive defines the symbol foo2 by setting aside sixteen bytes of storage space.

How Uninitialized Data Can Save File Space

Object files take advantage of the bss space saving concept. bss data in object files is represented as a size; not as the actual bytes of data. When an executable file is created by the linker, the bss sections are merged with the data sections and at this point, in the executable file, bss sections are transformed to zero-initial value data sections. (Note: some implementations leave the bss section in the executable file. But this means that it is the system loader's responsibility to zero out the bss section as it is created in memory. Whether the zero data transformation of the bss section is performed by the system loader or the linker, is an implementation decision based on performance criteria. The examples in this handbook assume that the linker transforms the bss section to a zero value data section.)

Studying Assembler Code

You should understand that this chapter has touched upon only the most cogent of COFF related functions associated with the UNIX assembler. Be prepared to find implementation-dependent, and reality driven, deviations from the generic tutorial presented here. For instance, the following example points out some of these deviations:

```
address    opcode            source            comments
-------    ------            ------            --------
                            .globl me      # external declaration
                            .text          # start text section
0000       03000000000c  call me           # opcode = 0300
0006       02000000000c  add   number, r0   # opcode = 0200

                            .data          # start data section
000c       00000004      number: .double 4 # data definition
```

In this example, note that the address column shows the first address in the data section to be simply one greater than the previous address in the text section. In reality this may not always be the case. The assembler might align the data section to some predetermined implementation dependent value. Typically, this value represents a 4-byte boundary. The example, coincidentally, does have the data section starting at a 4-byte boundary and being contiguous to the text section.

Also note that the address column represents the cumulative bytes used, and not bytes used per current section. This may not be the case in reality. Most assemblers display the current section byte count instead of the cumulative byte count. If this was the case in the example generic UNIX assembler, the address of the data section would be displayed as 0000 instead of 000c. Even if the section count is displayed, the opcode encoding probably is not changed and still references the symbol number at address 0000000c.

Another thing to keep in mind is that the .text assembler directive can appear any number of times in the source, but this does not mean that the COFF file contains that number of text sections. UNIX assemblers typically create only one text section, irrespective of the number of .text assembler directives. This is because the .text directive tells the assembler to start using the text section location counter. It does not mean to create another text section. This same logic applies to data and bss sections. Also you can't assume that the source sequence of .text, .data and .bss directives determines the order of these sections in the COFF file.

Lastly, and rather surprisingly, don't expect that all UNIX system assemblers can generate an assembly source listing. Some can't. And as for the occasional hedging used in this chapter's explanations, it is necessary because so much is implementation dependent. However, by the time you finish the rest of this handbook, you should be quite capable of dealing with the hedges as they might pertain to the UNIX implementation you are working with.

The Basics of COFF

The Assembly Code Relocation Process

COFF File Headers

Relocation Structures/Relocation Process

The Linking Process

The COFF System in UNIX

Magic Numbers

The COFF Symbolic Debug System

COFF and Shared Libraries

Utilities and Techniques for Working with COFF Files

A Sample COFF Program

3

COFF File Headers

COFF Mnemonics
The File Header
The Optional Header
COFF Structure File Pointers
File Header Summary

The roughly fifty or so bytes at the beginning of the COFF file contain the COFF file headers. The COFF file headers hold, among other things, the information indicating whether or not a file is executable and general run-time parameters. The headers are also the beginning point for the system of pointers that relate the different structures of the COFF file.

There are two COFF headers; both are defined as structures that contain pertinent COFF information fields. The first is called the **file header**, and the second (which may or may not be present) is called the **optional header**.

This chapter describes the contents of the header structures, the role they play in the COFF system, and how to use file pointers to access the various portions of a COFF file.

COFF Mnemonics

Since COFF headers are defined as structures, it is convenient to talk about them using their actual C language structure declarations, and to refer to the fields by their mnemonics. This is the common approach in UNIX COFF documentation, and quite reasonable since the C language COFF structure declarations are provided in source form on all UNIX System V machines.

The C language declarations for the COFF headers, as well as the rest of the COFF structure, are contained in **dot h** files (C language header include files) located in the */usr/include* directory.

The File Header

The first of the two COFF headers is usually simply referred to as the **file header** and contains general information such as a file time stamp and a magic number. Its structure declaration is found in the file *filehdr.h.*

File Header Structure

Looking into file *filehdr.h* you find the following declaration for the `filehdr` structure:

```
struct filehdr
{
    unsigned short   f_magic;    /* magic number */
    unsigned short   f_nscns;    /* number of sections */
    long             f_timdat;   /* time & date stamp */
    long             f_symptr;   /* file pointer to symtab */
    long             f_nsyms;    /* number of symtab entries */
    unsigned short   f_opthdr;   /* sizeof(optional hdr) */
    unsigned short   f_flags;    /* flags */
};

#define    FILHDR   struct filehdr
#define    FILHSZ   sizeof(FILHDR)
```

Unsigned short is a 16-bit (two-byte) value. Long is used for 32-bit (four-byte) values. Long is used instead of int for 32-bit values because that is the only data type in C that can currently be guaranteed to be 32-bits. This is because some machines implement int as 32-bits; others as 16-bits, but long, by C language definition, must be larger than int, so as it turns out today, long is the universal 32-bit value (at least for micro and mini-computers). Who knows what will happen when the new generation of 64-bit machines start to appear.

File Header Fields

File header fields have the following uses (see also Figure 3-1):

f_magic   identifies the particular UNIX implementation (or port) in which the COFF file was created. This magic number is discussed fully in Chapter 7.

f_nscns   represents the total number of **section headers**. Each section—text, data, bss, and some not yet introduced—is described by the information in its respective section header. Section headers follow the second COFF header and, like the COFF headers, represent a structure. Since the structure is a fixed length, all that is needed is the number of sections in order to write some code that can sequentially loop through the information in all the sections. Section headers are described in detail in the next chapter. But for now, simply note that the contents of a section (its **raw data**—machine code for a text section, program data for a data section) are separate from the respective section header.

f_timdat   is a time value in the standard UNIX time stamp format, which represents the number of seconds since 00:00:00 GMT (Greenwich Mean Time), January 1, 1970. This time value is not the same as seen when doing a long listing (the *ls –l* command) of a file. That time is maintained by the system and is part of the file's i-node structure. The COFF time-stamp is maintained by the various utilities that modify the COFF file. No general assumption should be made as to the consistency of this field's maintenance. For example, some linkers set this field when a executable file is created; some do not.

The *ctime*(3C) function is used to convert a UNIX time stamp into a readable ASCII string. When setting the time, the *time*(2) function is used to get the number of seconds since 00:00:00 GMT. See the source code in Chapter 11 for an example showing time access.

f_symptr   is a file pointer to the start of the symbol table. The contents and use of the symbol table information is covered in the next chapter, and in Chapter 8.

f_nsyms   is the number of symbol table entries. This value, along with the symbol table pointer, is used to write code that sequentially loops through the symbol table information.

f_opthdr   is the number of bytes in the second COFF header. Since the second COFF header is contiguous with the first, this value is used to find the first section header (section headers follow the second COFF header). The size of the second header is not a constant. This second header is commonly called the **optional header**; it is implementation-dependent and can be as large, or small, as required by a particular UNIX port. Also, many assemblers do not create an optional header, and therefore set this field to zero.

f_flags   is a boolean field representing the presence, or absence, of special COFF information, and the general state of the COFF file. The four least significant bits are found, and used, by virtually all implementations of COFF. The remaining twelve bits have meanings that vary between the UNIX ports.

The f_flags Field

The f_flags field is maintained primarily by the linker, and indicates special actions the linker may have taken on the COFF file. The following section presents the fields by the *filehdr.h* mnemonics. The flag values, all presented in octal, can be used as masks in a bitwise AND operation to determine if the flag is set. If the flag is set, its corresponding state is true for the COFF file.

F_RELFLG   (= 0000001) means the COFF file does not contain relocation information. This is normally true only for executable files. However, the linker has the ability to partially link object files and produce an output file that can
be used as input to the linker for a subsequent link. If an
object file is linked with the linker's retain option set,
the linker does not set this flag.

F_EXEC   (= 0000002) if the file is executable. The linker sets this
flag when all external symbolic addresses have been
resolved.

F_LNNO   (= 0000004) if line numbers have been stripped from the
COFF file. Line numbers are part of the COFF system's
debug information, and are covered in detail in Chapter
8's discussion on the COFF symbolic debug system.
This field is used by symbolic debuggers to determine
whether source-level debug is possible. Line numbers
become part of the COFF file when source is compiled
with debug information. Line numbers are removed
either by the linker, which has an option to do this, or by
the *strip*(1) utility. COFF files are usually stripped once
they are released for general use since the stripping of
debug information greatly reduces the size of the file.

L_SYMS   (= 0000010) if local symbols have been stripped from
the COFF file. What is meant by local symbols is best
explained by example. The C library, *libc.a*, is a collec-
tion of object files that link with your application.
External symbolic references (declarations) in your
application are matched with each symbol's definition in
libc.a. These matching symbols in *libc.a* are global
symbols, and they must be present in the COFF symbol
table in order for the linker resolution process to work.
All other symbols are local and can be stripped from the
COFF file to reduce the size. The linker has an option to
do this. When used, the result is an object file suitable
for linking but containing no superfluous information.
The details of this process are explained in Chapter 8's
discussion on the COFF symbolic debug system.

The remaining bits in the `f_flags` field are implementation-dependent. The best place to find the specifics is in the file *filehdr.h* on your UNIX system, or your system specific COFF Programmer's Guide (if it is available). Hopefully, the documentation reflects port-specific uses of `f_flags` bits. Do not ignore these bits and assume that setting them to zero is the safe and easy thing to do. Most UNIX implementations use some of these bits to check the COFF file's identity, and as an extra safety measure to insure that the COFF file is not corrupted, or from a foreign system. Other uses of these bits include flagging the presence of special system hardware, or to flag special processing needs.

The Optional Header

The second COFF header is known by at least four names: optional header, standard header, system a.out header, and auxiliary header. This handbook chooses to call the second header the **optional header** for two good reasons: first, it is an appropriate name because it describes the header's purpos—to hold optional, implementation-dependent and run-time dependent information; and second, the most recent UNIX System V documentation uses optional header more frequently than the other names. But be warned that the COFF developers indulged in the multi-name confusion by naming the optional-header structure declaration file *aouthdr.h*.

The Optional Header Structure

Most of the fields in the optional header provide run-time information about the COFF file. And since only executable files need run-time information, it is the linker that fills in the appropriate values. Typically, assembler-created object files do not contain the optional header, but if the optional header is present, most of its values are meaningless (and not necessarily initialized to zero).

The *aouthdr.h* file declares the following fields for the optional header:

```
typedef struct aouthdr
{
      short magic;        /* magic number                       */
      short vstamp;       /* version stamp                      */
      long  tsize;        /* text size in bytes                 */
      long  dsize;        /* initialized data size              */
      long  bsize;        /* uninitialized data  size           */
      long  entry;        /* entry point                        */
      long  text_start;   /* base of text used for this file    */
      long  data_start;   /* base of data used for this file    */
} AOUTHDR;
```

Optional Header Fields

Optional header fields have the following meanings and uses (see also Figure 3-2 for how the various fields of the optional header relate to the corresponding executable file's image in memory):

magic   establishes the state of the COFF file. The most common value for magic is 0413 (octal) which indicates that the COFF file is a **normal executable file.** Normal executable files have the following characteristics: all machine code is contained in one text section, all data is contained in one data section (during the process of creating an executable file, the linker consolidates the text, data, and bss sections of the individual object files into one large text section, and one large data section that also contains the bss section); the data section follows the text section; both are aligned to suitable address boundaries as dictated by architecture's paging mechanism; and the text section is write-protected. Other implementation-dependent values are usually documented in file the *a.out.h* in the */usr/include* directory.

Contrast the meaning of this **magic** number with the **file header** f_magic number, which indicates the particular UNIX port or environment of the COFF file.

vstamp This value is usually set by the assembler and used by the linker to check for object file backward—or forward—compatibility. This field is totally implementation-dependent; some implementations do not use it; some linkers allow you to specify a custom vstamp value for the linker's output file.

The remaining six fields provide necessary run-time information that is used by the kernel to load and execute the program. These fields contain valid values only for normal executable files.

Normal executable files are created by the **default link process**. For example, if you `cc` a source file, the C compiler driver invokes the linker which supplies the default optional header values, and the resulting *a.out* file can readily execute on the system. The default optional header can be changed by writing a linker directive file that changes the appropriate fields.

The last six fields of the optional header have the following uses and meanings:

tsize
is the size of the text section. Text section size is almost always rounded upward to the next 4-byte boundary value. If a linker directive file forces the linker to create multiple text sections in the linker's output file, the true meaning of `tsize` can be determined only by experimentation. Expect it to represent only the size of the first text section.

dsize
is the size of the data section. And just as the text section size can be affected by special linker directives, so too can the data section be affected in the same way. If more than one data section is present in an executable file, expect `dsize` to represent only the size of the first data section.

bsize
is the size of the uninitialized data, the bss section. Though this is typically a legitimate value, it is not used by the system loader since the bss section is consolidated with the data section. Most systems do this because it results in faster program initialization. When bss is changed into zero-value-initialized data in the data section, the kernel loading and paging mechanism is simpler, and simpler means less overhead.

entry
is the address used by the system as the starting point for program execution. Rarely, if ever, is this address the same as the start of the text section. The linker sets the entry point to the address of the symbol `_start`. `_start` is defined in the appropriate C

run-time file (*crt0.o* for V.2; *crt1.o* for V.3; found in directory */lib*).

Normal executable files are always linked with a C run-time file, so normal executables always have the symbol `_start`. However, if the executable is not created normally, it is possible that a C run-time file has not been used, and the linker will not find the symbol `_start`. Instead the linker then looks for the symbol `_main`, which corresponds to a C program's `main()` function. (C source language symbols are all prefixed with an underscore in the corresponding assembly source, and since the linker uses assembly source created object files, the C source `main` symbol is actually `_main`) If `_main` is not found, the `entry` field is usually set to zero, but this treatment is not consistent for all UNIX linkers. The entry can also be set to a symbol you specify by using a linker command line option intended for this purpose (not all UNIX linkers have this feature).

`text_start`   is the start address of the text section. The default start address is usually some architecturally-determined and paging-mechanism-implementation-dependent value. And, of course, linker directives can greatly affect this value. As a matter of fact, use of linker directives can virtually guarantee a change in this value.

`data_start`   is the start address of the data section. Like the text_start value, it is bound to be affected if the default link process is altered by linker directives.

Using Optional Header Information

Linker directives are used to create special purpose object and executable files. A common special enhancement is to support cross-development projects by providing object and executable files that are suitable for firmware applications. You now know enough about the the optional header to intelligently approach this type of enhancement. For example, suppose you are writing a utility that downloads program code to a PROM programmer. PROM programmers usually require an offset value that is used to adjust the memory range of the downloaded code into the range of the PROM. The `text_start` value can be used in part, or in whole, as the offset value.

Also remember that the optional header described here contains only what might be considered the universal fields, and that in reality you might find any number of implementation-dependent fields. Most common implementation-dependent fields are padding fields whose purpose is to force the start of the section headers to some boundary value that improves file-seek positioning efficiency.

COFF Structure File Pointers

This section explains the meaning of file pointer as it pertains to the COFF structure.

File pointers play the central role in accessing the various structures within the COFF file. This is a good point to take the time to learn what file pointers are and how to use them.

File Pointer Value

A COFF file pointer's value represents a byte offset into the COFF file. For example, if `f_symptr`, the pointer to the start of the symbol table, has a value of 2000 (decimal), the symbol table starts at byte 2000 in the COFF file. File byte-offset values used in UNIX start at zero. The **file header**, the first structure of the COFF file, therefore, starts at byte 0 of the COFF file. See Figure 3-1 for an illustration of the use of the `f_symptr` value.

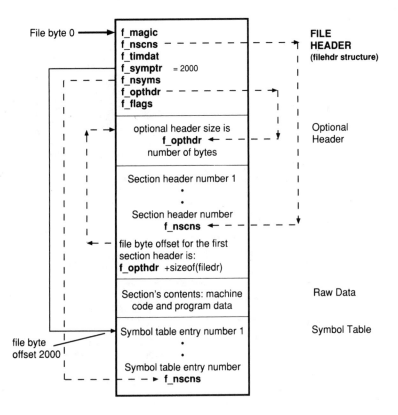

Figure 3-1. File header components and structural relationships

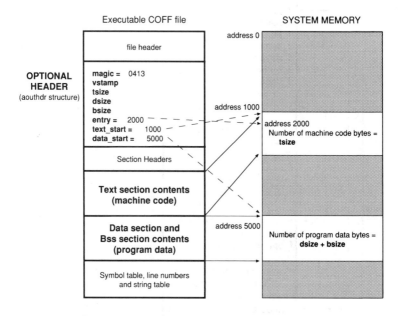

This diagram shows how the various fields in the optional header are used in mapping the executable file's image into system memory. Typically, the optional header fields are meaningful only for executable files.

Figure 3-2. The executable COFF file in memory

File pointer values can be used with several C library functions that provide file I/O support. For example, the following C code shows how to quickly and easily prepare for reading the symbol table:

```
fseek( fd, fhd.f_symptr, 0 )
```

fhd is a FILHDR variable type, easily defined by using the respective #define macro in the file *filehdr.h*. The fseek function positions the file pointer of the file associated with file descriptor fd to the start of the symbol table. The third argument, 0, indicates that the file byte-offset value passed to fseek is to be interpreted relative to the start of the file. All initial fseeks that use a COFF file pointer must use 0 as the third argument to fseek.

A properly argumented *fread* function can now read the first symbol table entry. In general, the COFF header (dot h) files contain structure declarations and useful macro definitions that make dealing with the complexities of COFF quite simple.

Chapter 11 contains a number of comprehensive C source code examples that demonstrate how to access the various portions of a COFF file.

File Header Summary

The following is a brief summary of the COFF structure.

- The COFF structure begins with two headers:
  a. The **file header**
  b. The **optional header**
- **Section headers** follow the optional header. The position of the first section header is found by adding the size of the filehdr structure to the value found in the f_opthdr field that represent the size of the optional header.
- In general, the **file header** is the starting point for gaining access to the rest of the COFF file since it contains such relevant information as:

    a. f_nscns, the number of sections.

    b. nsyms and f_symptr symbol table access information.

- The file header magic number, f_magic, describes the COFF file's UNIX environment.

- The optional header magic number, magic, describes the COFF file's state or condition.

- The optional header, in general, contains program run-time information that has been set by the linker. Usually, assembler-created object files do not have an optional header. The optional header is usually created by the linker.

The Basics of COFF

The Assembly Code
Relocation Process

COFF File Headers

Relocation Structures/
Relocation Process

The Linking Process

The COFF System in UNIX

Magic Numbers

The COFF Symbolic
Debug System

COFF and Shared Libraries

Utilities and Techniques for
Working with COFF Files

A Sample COFF Program

4

Relocation Structures/ Relocation Process

Section Headers
Relocation Entries
Relocation Entry Values
Symbol Table Entries
Symbol Table Entry Values
How Relocated Addresses Are Calculated
COFF Up to Here

Relocation makes COFF object files extremely flexible. Because of relocation, an object file is not bound to any particular address space: it is **address-space-independent**. For this reason, object files are often referred to explicitly as **relocatable object** files, or simply **relocatable** files.

The advantages of relocation are quite obvious, especially for applications that consist of many object files. If it were not for relocation, the consideration of individual object file address spaces as they relate to the final executable image would present a nightmarish calculation and logistical problem. A less obvious advantage of relocation is the characterization of program addressing modes as a function of a software defined structure as opposed to any particular hardware imposed addressing requirements. In this sense, the concept of relocation is one of the key elements of the COFF definition's hardware-to-software transformation.

There are three COFF structures that implement the relocation process: section headers, relocation entries, and symbol table entries. These three structures work together to define the areas in machine code and data that require patching with run-time addresses.

Section Headers

The section header contains two fields that play a key role in the process of relocation: s_relptr, the pointer to the relocation entries; and s_scnptr, the pointer to the sections raw data.

During the following discussion, you'll find it helpful to look at Figure 4-1.

The Section Header Structure

The **section header**'s structural declaration is found in file *scnhdr.h* and describes all of the vital section characteristics.

Looking at file *scnhdr.h*, you find the following structure declaration:

```
struct scnhdr {
    char            s_name[8];/* section name */
    long            s_paddr;  /* physical address */
    long            s_vaddr;  /* virtual address */
    long            s_size;   /* section size */
    long            s_scnptr; /* file ptr to raw data for section */
    long            s_relptr; /* file ptr to relocation */
    long            s_lnnoptr;/* file ptr to line numbers */
    unsigned short  s_nreloc; /* number of relocation entries */
    unsigned short  s_nlnno;  /* number of line number entries */
    long            s_flags;  /* type and content flags */
    };

#define SCNHDR struct scnhdr
#define SCNHSZ sizeof(SCNHDR)
```

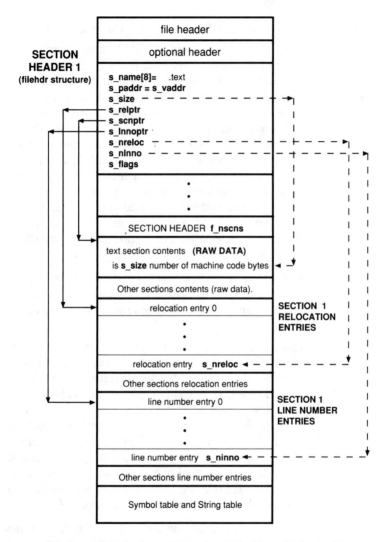

This diagram illustrates the use of the various fields of the section header. The section shown in this example is a text section. The usage of the fields is analogous for the data section. However, since the bss section does not have raw data, relocation entries, and line numbers, has those relevant fields set to zero.

Figure 4-1. Section header schema

Section Header Fields

Section header fields have the following meanings and uses:

s_name   is an eight-byte null-padded ASCII string representing the section name. This field is set by the assembler. The name is either the same as one of the section creating assembler directives (**.text**, **.data**, or **.bss**), or is defined by the assembler's **.section** directive. Some special section names that can appear include: **.init**, **.lib** and **.comment**. The first two are associated with **shared libraries** and are discussed in Chapter 9, *COFF and Shared Libraries*; the comment section contains copyright notices and other software administrative trivia. (**.ident** assembler directive is used to put entries into the comment section. The argument to the `.ident` directive is a character string that is concatenated to the COFF file's comment section.)

Linker directive action can change the section name, and the section's name does not necessarily represent its contents, since that too can be changed by linker directives.

s_paddr   and s_vaddr represent the physical (start) address of the section and the virtual (start) address of the section. Though the section header structure discriminates between the two, in reality these two fields always contain the same value. This is because of the way memory mapping is handled by the UNIX system. The application program does not need to know its physical address; in fact, modern memory management systems make it impossible for the application to know, and therefore the distinction is irrelevant. The virtual-physical distinction is completely transparent to the application.

Current UNIX COFF documentation introduces some confusion on this issue since COFF documentation makes reference to both virtual and physical addresses. To resolve this confusion, just remember that in COFF, virtual is synonymous with physical; and the best way to conceptually visualize an application program's address space is simply as that area defined by the linker. If you are interested in actual numerical values for the linker-defined address space, the best thing to do is compile and link a small C program and have the linker produce an **output map** of the executable file. This handbook uses the term **address** to refer to application address space as defined by the linker.

s_size   is the size in bytes of the section's contents. (For example, a text section's size is the number of bytes of machine code.) Size is almost always padded upward to the next 4-byte boundary value.

s_scnptr   is a file pointer to the section's contents, or **raw data** as it is commonly referred to in COFF documentation. It is called raw data because no processing is needed. When loaded by the system, raw data appears byte for byte in memory exactly as it appears in the section's raw data area in the executable file.

You may be asking, "What about the bss section? I thought it was created especially because it has no raw data." You're right. The meaning of s_scnptr for the bss section is discussed in Section Types in Chapter 6. Also remember that this file pointer, like all COFF structure file pointers, can be used directly as the file position argument for the **fseek** function.

s_relptr   is the file pointer to the relocation information. Recall that a machine code's address encoding for a reference to data in the data section results in an address value that is eventually modified by the linker in accordance with the program's run-time memory mapping, and that the information indicating the necessity of link-time address modification is contained in the **relocation information** area of the COFF file. This is the pointer to the area containing relocation information. Each section has its own relocation information. Relocation information is a sequence of structures. The details of the relocation structure are covered later in this chapter.

s_lnnoptr   is a pointer to the COFF line number structure. The line number structure is part of the COFF symbolic debug system and is covered in Chapter 8.

s_nreloc   and s_nlnno represent the number of relocation structures (entries) and the number of line number structures
(entries) respectively for this section. These values are
used to implement loops that sequentially process their
respective information.

s_flags   bits represent two kinds of information:

   • section handling

   • section contents

The s_flags determine how the linker and system
loader handle the section. Section handling and contents
are described in detail in Chapter 6.

Relocation Entries

A relocation entry is created by the assembler for every instance of an
address reference that requires patching by the linker.

The Relocation Structure

The file *reloc.h* contains the relocation structure's declaration as follows:

```
struct reloc {
    long            r_vaddr;  /* address of reference */
    long            r_symndx; /* index into symbol table */
    unsigned short  r_type;   /* relocation type */
    };
```

Relocation Entry Fields

Relocation entry fields implement the dynamics of relocation. The
reloc structure fields play the following roles in the process of relocation:

- The r_vaddr field is the backbone of the relocation system. The r_vaddr value represents the area in the raw data that requires **patching** by the linker. The r_vaddr value is a byte-offset value relative to the start of its raw data, and typically points to that area in raw data that is the machine instruction's encoding for the address reference.

- The r_symndx value is a pointer to the appropriate symbol table entry that contains run-time address information. The symbol table entry is accessed by adding this value, r_symndx, to the value of f_symptr in the filehdr structure. (See the Section "The File Header" in Chapter 3.) The symbol table entry's address is easily calculated using the C language's pointer arithmetic ability. For example, the current symbol table entry's address is easily found by the following C code:

```
current_symptr = F_symptr + reloc.r_symndx;
```

NOTE

Use this approach with caution. Pointers have to be declared or defined properly. For this code to work, both F_symptr and current_symptr must be declared/defined as pointers to syment, the symbol table information structure. As an alternate to the pointer arithmetic method, it is possible to ignore associative declarations and force the correct calculation by multiplying the r_symndx by sizeof(syment) and then adding that to F_symptr. Before using the C sizeof function, always check the COFF header files for possible defines of the structure's size for those cases where sizeof might return an incorrect value due to structure padding. Use defined sizes if present. Chapter 10 has a number of helpful guidelines on the programming-style topics briefly covered here. Chapter 11 has a number of comprehensive source code examples that demonstrate the use of file-pointers and defined types.

- The r_type tells the linker what type of addressing mode must be used. This field differentiates between absolute addresses versus program-counter relative addresses, in effect telling the linker which algorithm to use during the address calculation process. This field is completely implementation dependent. Some implementations use only a few addressing modes; others use over a dozen. The file *reloc.h* contains implementation-dependent r_type definitions.

Relocation Entry Values

The relocation structure's field values identify the area in raw data that needs patching and associates that area with a symbol table entry that defines the run-time address—the value used to patch the raw data.

The example in this section is used to explain the details behind relocation entry values.

Relocatable Code Dynamics

Consider the following assembly code example:

```
address   opcode              source          comments
-------   ------              ------          --------
                              .globl me       # external declaration
                              .text           # start text section
0000      030000000000  call  me              # opcode = 0300
0006      020000000040  add   number, r0      # opcode = 0200
000c      030000000020  call  it              # opcode = 0300
                                 .
                                 .
                              it:             # routine "it"
0020      020000000040  add   number, r0      # defined here
                                              # its code
                                 .
                                 .
                              ret             # return

                              .data           # start data section
0040      00000004    number: .double 4       # data definition
```

Note the emboldened areas in the opcode. These represent the sections of the machine code that are patched by the linker with the run-time address. Each of these symbolic references cause the assembler to create a relocation entry. The first relocation entry, created as a result of the `call me` instruction, has the following information:

```
struct reloc {
    long             r_vaddr  = 2
    long             r_symndx = 0  /* for symbol "me" */
    unsigned short   r_type   = 0
} reloc_1st;
```

The simple example CPU has only one addressing mode—absolute; therefore, the `r_type` is always zero (and is not shown explicitly in other examples).

The `r_vaddr` has a value of 2 because, in the text section's raw data, the second byte (byte count starts at 0) is the start of the 32-bit (four-byte) address encoding that is the `call` instruction's destination.

The value for `r_symndx` is 0 because the symbol me is the first symbolic declaration in the source file (the `.globl me`), and therefore, the first entry in the symbol table.

This relocation entry is associated with the first symbol table entry because the `call` instruction references the symbol me , and the symbol table entry for me contains the information that eventually is used by the linker to determine the actual address of me .

The assembler creates a symbol table entry for every symbol. The `.globl me` is a symbolic declaration that goes into the symbol table as entry 0 (indexing starts at 0). The `.text` is also a symbol (in addition to telling the assembler to start a text section), and therefore has a symbol table entry. The `.text` symbol is the second entry in the symbol table. The definition of the symbol it is the third symbol table entry, the `.data` directive is the fourth symbol table entry, and the definition of the symbol number is the fifth symbol table entry.

NOTE

The simple, serial sequence of symbol table entries used in the example simplifies the relocation/symbol process explanation, but does not represent the actual sequence of symbols in a COFF file. In reality, the symbol table sequence follows very rigid, predefined sequence rules. These rules are covered in Chapter 8.

The second relocation entry, created for the

```
        add number, r0
```

source line, has the following information:

```
struct reloc {
        long        r_vaddr  = 8
        long        r_symndx = 3   /* for symbol ".data" */
        } reloc_2nd;
```

The r_vaddr value is 8, because the second instruction's encoding for the referenced datum starts at byte eight in the raw data; this is no surprise. However, r_symndx is the symbol table entry for .data , not for the symbol number in the data section. How this works is explained shortly.

These two relocation cases completely describe the relocation process: no further examples are needed. Why? Because:

- External data symbolic references are handled and processed in the same manner as external routine symbolic references. Both cases simply represent an address defined in some other object file.

- An intra-section symbolic reference is handled and processed in the same manner as an inter-section symbolic address, except that the relocation entry symbol index is associated with the section's own symbol table entry. For example, the call it instruction's relocation entry r_symndx is 1, the symbol table entry for .text .

This generalization does carry one caveat: it can be implementation dependent. Some implementations might use a far more complex system, but even so, prior to understanding a specific complex instance, an understanding of the simple fundamentals is required.

Symbol Table Entries

Though the symbol table entry is not an excessively large structure, the information it contains is the most complex of the COFF definition. This is because of the complex nature of debug information. All symbols have a symbol table entry, but not all have relocation information.

COFF defines a dual role for the symbol table: defining the run-time address for the relocation process, and providing symbolic debug information. For the moment debug information aspect is ignored and instead the explanation concentrates only on those parts of the symbol table entry that play a role in the relocation process.

Symbol Table Structure

The symbol table structure contains information that determines the symbol's address—the value that the linker patches into the raw data.

The symbol table structure is declared in file *syms.h*. The four fields that are used by the relocation process are shown in bold type:

```
struct syment
{
  union
  {
      char   _n_name[SYMNMLEN];/* Symbol name */
      struct                   /* if _n_name[0-3] == 0 */
          {
          long _n_zeroes;      /* then _n_name[4-7] is an  */
          long _n_offset;      /* offset into string table */
          } _n_n;
      char  *_n_nptr[2];       /* allows for overlaying */
  } _n;
  long            n_value;     /* value of symbol */
  short           n_scnum;     /* section number */
  unsigned short  n_type;      /* type and derived type */
  char            n_sclass;    /* storage class */
  char            n_numaux;    /* number of aux. entries */
};
```

Symbol Table Entry Fields

Symbol table entry fields have the following meanings and uses:

The _n_name field holds the symbol's name. This field is important for the resolution of external symbolic references since the defining symbol is matched by name. The _n_name field is also used to identify symbolic information for the special sections: text, data, and bss.

The n_value can contain the address of the symbol. This can be the value that the linker uses to patch symbolic address references. In other words, this value is placed into the area in the section's raw data pointed to by the relocation structure's r_vaddr value.

Contrast the role of r_vaddr to the role of the symbol table entry's n_value. Whereas r_vaddr tells the linker where in raw data to **patch** in the run-time calculated address, the symbol table entry contains a field that tells the linker what value to patch it to.

How n_value is interpreted depends on its **storage class**. The n_sclass field contains the storage class. There are over twenty different storage classes, and most of them deal with some sort of symbolic debug information, as will be seen in Chapter 8. But for now, only two storage classes are of interest: C_EXT, external symbol storage, and C_STAT, static symbol storage. Both of these storage classes represent a relocatable address—therefore, the n_value is something the linker must contend with. (The C_EXT and C_STAT mnemonics, and others, are found in the files *syms.h* and *storclass.h*, and are used as the shorthand terminology in this handbook wherever appropriate.)

n_scnum is the section number where the symbol is defined. (The section where storage space is allocated for it.)

Symbol Table Entry Values

Symbol table entries that are used for the relocation process are differentiated from those used only for debug information by certain values in the symbol table entry.

This section describes the symbol table values used for the relocation process by expanding on the relocation structure examples shown in the Relocatable Code Dynamics Section of this chapter. The example expansion associates a symbol table entry with its respective relocation entry. Also, it might be helpful to reference Figure 4-2 as you read through the following section.

Relocation-process Symbol Table Entries

Referring back to the example in the Relocatable Code Dynamics Section, the first relocation entry, created as a result of the `call me` instruction's external symbolic reference, has the following information:

```
struct reloc {
        long        r_vaddr  = 2
        long        r_symndx = 0   /* for symbol "me" */
        } reloc_1st;
```

The first entry in the symbol table (`r_symndx` = 0), has the following values:

```
struct syment {
        unsigned long   n_value  =  0
        short           n_scnum  =  0
        char            n_sclass = C_EXT
        } syment_0
```

Since this is a symbolic reference to an external symbol, the symbol's address is unknown, and also unknown is the section where the symbol is defined. The symbolic entry associated with this relocation entry describes this situation of unknowns by setting the storage class (`n_sclass`) to `C_EXT` (external symbol), and `n_value` to zero. (An `n_value` of 0 with `n_sclass` of `C_EXT` does not imply address 0.) And `n_scnum` is also zero, meaning that the section where me is defined is unknown. Note that section numbering starts at 1. Section number zero, and negative values, have special meanings described in Chapter 8. How the linker uses `C_EXT` symbol table entry information is described in Chapter 5.

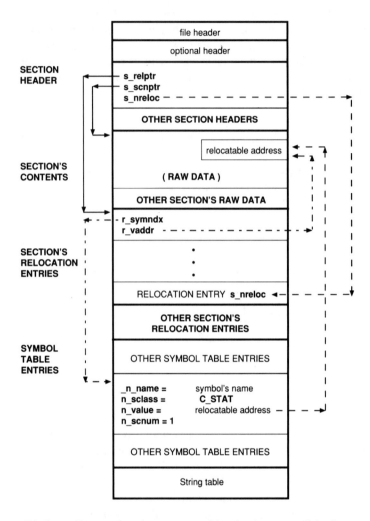

This diagram illustrates the major components of the relocation system. Notice the different uses for the pointer field values. For example, r_vaddr is a byte offset relative to the start of the section's contents, and points to the area in raw data that is relocated (patched). r_symndx is an index value into the symbol table. On the other hand, s_scnptr is a file pointer to the start of the section's raw data.

Figure 4-2. Relocation system components

The second relocation entry from the example is created for the add number, r0 source line, and has the following information:

```
struct reloc {
     long          r_vaddr  = 8
     long          r_symndx = 3   /* for symbol ".data" */
} reloc_2nd;
```

This relocation entry is associated with the fourth symbol table entry. The fourth entry in the symbol table, (r_symndx = 3) has the following values:

```
struct syment {
        unsigned long    n_value  =  40
        short            n_scnum  =  2
        char             n_sclass = C_STAT
} syment_3
```

A storage class of C_STAT means that the n_value is a **relocatable address**, a value that is processed by the linker and set to reflect an actual run-time address. The value of n_value is 40 (hex), the start of the data section, and n_scnum is 2, since the data section is the second section (text is 1) and defines itself.

Recall that this relocation structure is created as a result of a reference to a datum in the data section, yet the symbol table entry associated with this relocation structure points to the .data symbol table entry. This association works because of the way relocation entries are processed. The run-time, or relocated address, can be calculated by using the start address of the section, the n_value, and the value of the address reference as found by an indirect reference through r_vaddr. This type of processing is more efficient (less data structure manipulation) than setting r_symndx to the symbol table entry for the symbol itself. The general rule followed by the relocation process is to set the r_symndx to the symbol table entry for the section where the symbol is defined, and to get the symbol's relative offset in the section by using the address in the raw data. This process is clearly explained in the next section. Chapter 6 explains how the linker uses relocation information to resolve external references.

How Relocated Addresses Are Calculated

This section presents a step-by-step walkthrough of a simple relocation process.

Simple relocation is performed on C_STAT storage class symbols. The C_STAT storage class derives its name from the C language **static** variable. The word static in C implies **privacy**, limited scope, and/or regionalism. C_STAT symbols are symbols that have a defined relocatable address, (a meaningful n_value), as opposed to a C_EXT symbol whose n_value is 0 because its address is unknown. C_STAT symbols are usually defined in the current source file, and in that sense they have a source file regionalism, limited scope, and privacy.

The simple relocation case occurs only when one source file is compiled and linked. This is not very realistic, since most applications consist of several source files that have external symbolic references. Though lacking realism, the simple relocation case is the best way to explain the basics of the relocation process.

Relocatable Code Before Linking

The following example shows address encoding of a machine code symbolic access to data defined in the data section:

```
address    opcode          source            comments
-------    ------          ------            --------
                           .text            # start text section
0000       030000000000    call  me         # opcode = 0300
0006       020000000040    add   number, r0 # opcode = 0200
                             .
                             .

                           .data            # start data section
0040       00000004        number: .double 4 # data definition
```

The object file created by the assembler results in the add number, r0 instruction finding number at address 40 (hex). That instruction's machine code encoding for number's address is 40 (the emboldened portion of the opcode).

Linking this object file causes the relocation process to be performed. For the moment, assume that linked executable files have the text section starting at 0, and the data section starting at 100 (hex). This means that the linker updates (or relocates) the add number, r0 instruction's symbolic reference to number with the correct runtime address.

The add number, r0 source line has the following relocation/ symbol information:

```
struct reloc {
    long        r_vaddr  = 8
    long        r_symndx = 3   /* for symbol ".data" */
} reloc_2nd;

struct syment {
    unsigned long  n_value  =  40
    short          n_scnum  =  2
    char           n_sclass =  C_STAT
        } syment_3
```

Linker Algorithms

How the linker calculates the relocated address is illustrated by the following pseudo-algorithms:

```
run_time_sec_addr = 0x100;                            /* step 1 */
reloc_addr       = get_reloc_addr( r_vaddr );        /* step 2 */
sec_addr         = get_sec_addr( r_symndx );         /* step 3 */
reloc_addr       = reloc_addr - sec_addr;            /* step 4 */
reloc_addr       = reloc_addr + run_time_sec_addr;   /* 5 */
patch_reloc_addr  ( r_vaddr, reloc_addr);            /* step 6 */
```

These six steps perform the following:

1. The run_time_sec_addr is obvious. The linker sets the runtime start address of the data section.

2. The get_reloc_addr function returns the current relocation address from raw data as pointed to by r_vaddr. The current relocation address is 40 (hex). Though not shown for simplicity's sake, this function works with the section header's raw data pointer, s_scnptr.

3. Using the relocation entry's r_symndx value, this function returns the n_value from the symbol table entry. In this case n_value represents the section's current start address, 40 (hex).

4. The relative offset of the symbol within the section is calculated by taking the difference between the section's start address and the value of the relocatable address, which represents the symbol's address within the section. In this case the offset is 0, since number is the first datum defined in the data section.

5. The run-time address of the symbol number is its offset (0) plus the run-time start of the data section (100). In this case the address is 100 (hex).

6. All that's left to do is update the raw data. The patch_ reloc_addr function uses the runtime reloc_addr and the r_vaddr value to patch the machine code's address for number to the run-time value. The symbolic address reference to number is now **relocated**. The raw data machine code now has the run-time address encoded for the data reference.

Relocatable Code After Linking

The relocated code looks like this:

```
address    opcode           source           comments
-------    ------           ------           --------
                            .text            # start text section
0000       030000000000     call  me         # opcode = 0300
0006       020000000100     add   number, r0 # opcode = 0200

                            .data            # start data section
0100       00000004 number: .double 4        # data definition
```

Relocation is as simple as that. But, of course, real linkers don't use poor redundant coding as presented in the example, whose sole point was to clearly illustrate the process. The process also involves a little bit more than shown, such as checking storage class types and section numbers to make sure that the relocation/symbol information relations do indeed represent a relocatable address situation.

Relocation Process Summary

The entire relocation process represents an efficient interplay between relatively few structures and fields that effectively control relocation. The examples in this chapter are a simplification of the relocation process; a real implementation might be quite complex, but the complexity is simply a recursive application of the few simple ideas presented here, such as a relocation loop using s_nreloc value from the section header.

COFF Up to Here

At this point most of the COFF structure has been explained. The headers have been dealt with, as have the section headers, relocation entries, and symbol table entries. There are only two more COFF structures to cover: the string table, and the line number table.

The string table stores symbol names that are more than eight character long, and gives the C language its proverbial ability to support symbol names of any length.

The line number table provides debug information that is used to implement source flow-traced-debugging.

Both of these structures are detailed in Chapter 8 on the debug system.

The Basics of COFF

The Assembly Code Relocation Process

COFF File Headers

Relocation Structures/ Relocation Process

The Linking Process

The COFF System in UNIX

Magic Numbers

The COFF Symbolic Debug System

COFF and Shared Libraries

Utilities and Techniques for Working with COFF Files

A Sample COFF Program

5

The Linking Process

Multiple Source Files
Multiple File Relocation—Local References
Multiple File Relocation—External References
Relocation Process Summary

The linking process does much more than just simple relocation of local symbolic references. The linker's most important function is the resolution of external symbolic variables—external symbolic references cannot be avoided.

This chapter explains the following two very real conditions that the linker must deal with:

- Multiple files
- External symbolic references

Understanding how the linker handles these two conditions highlights some important relocation-process actions that can help you use the linker in a more efficient manner.

Multiple Source Files

In reality most applications consist of multiple source files. This implies multiple object files that must be merged into one final executable file by the linker. Even if an application is contained in one source file, this still means linking many object files, since at a minimum, the C library, *libc.a*, must be linked with the application object file. And this is a simple case. It's not unusual for an application to use several libraries, such as *libm.a*, the math library, or *libcurses.a*, the screen graphics library. Thousands of object files might be involved in the linking process!

This does not present a terrible problem to the linker. As a matter of fact, only one additional step prior to address relocation has to be performed. That step involves merging all of the text sections into one text section, and merging all of the data sections into one data section. The creation of the executable's data section also involves merging all of the bss sections with the data sections. Merged bss sections become data sections whose data is all zeroes. (Remember, for most implementations the executable file contains only one text section, and one data section.)

How the Linker Builds the Executable

A brief discussion of the linker's internal operation helps to understand how multiple object files are handled.

Input object files are processed one at a time, usually in the sequence they appear in the linker invocation command line. For example:

```
ld foo1.o foo2.o foo3.o -o foo
```

This invocation of the linker creates an output file named `foo` which is composed of the three input object files: `foo1.o`, `foo2.o`, and `foo3.o`. `foo1.o` is the first file processed.

Processing includes performing relocation and building a list (actually several) in memory that represent the contents of the output file. There are lists for section headers, relocation entries, symbol table entries, and every other component of the COFF structure. The output file is created in memory before it is written as a real file. By building the output file in memory, the linker has a great deal of flexibility in constructing any type of mapping. After all, memory (list) manipulations (such as insertions and deletions) are easy and efficient, as compared to the same operations on a file, which involve costly creations of temporary files and a great deal of sequential I/O. So, the important point to keep in mind is that in the following linker action examples, the output is actually being created in memory; not in the output file.

Multiple File Relocation—Local References

The processing of multiple object files involves just one additional step to the relocation process described in Chapter 4. This step is shown in the following linker action example:

```
run_time_sec_addr = 0x100;                               /* step 1 */
for ( n=1; n==NUMBER_OF_OBJECT_FILES ) {
    init_object_file_vars( n );

    for ( j=0; j==s_nreloc; j++ ) {
        reloc_addr     = get_reloc_addr( r_vaddr );   /* step 2 */
        sec_addr       = get_sec_addr( r_symndx );    /* step 3 */
        reloc_addr     = reloc_addr - sec_addr;       /* step 4 */
        reloc_addr     = reloc_addr + run_time_sec_addr; /*    5 */
        patch_reloc_addr  ( r_vaddr, reloc_addr );    /* step 6 */
        }

    run_time_sec_addr = run_time_sec_addr + s_size;   /* step 7 */
    }
```

The only difference between this example and the linker pseudo-code example in Chapter 4 (the "Linker Algorithms" section) is the addition of the outer for loop to perform the relocation process for n input object files.

The init_object_file_vars function sets the important pointers of the current object file. This includes setting up the section header values and header values such as: s_scnptr, pointer to raw data; s_relptr, pointer to relocation entries; f_symptr, pointer to symbol table; and f_nsyms, number of symbol table entries.

Multiple object file processing can be summarized as follows:

- Step 1 sets the start address for the first section.

- Subsequent section start addresses are simply calculated in step 7, by adding the size of the current section to the current start address to calculate the start address of the next section (which, of course, is in the next object file).

- Keep in mind that symbol table updating occurs (but is not explicitly shown in the action example).

Since the COFF definition is recursive, multiple object file processing is as easy to implement as making one' specific sequence of actions for one object file apply repeatedly for all object files until all object files are processed.

Multiple File Relocation—External References

The linker process of matching an external symbolic reference (a declaration) to the symbol's definition is known as resolution.

There are two sides to this process:

- The declaration side, usually the side making the symbolic reference.

- The definition side, the place where the symbol actually resides; where storage space is allocated for it.

The following example shows the important components of the declaration (reference) side of the source, and the resulting relocation and symbol table entries:

```
address   opcode         source         comments
-------   ------         ------         --------
                         .file  foo1
                         .globl me      # external declaration

                         .text          # start text section
0000   030000000000      call me            # opcode = 0300
```

```
struct reloc {
        long            r_vaddr  = 2
        long            r_symndx = 0   /* for symbol "me" */
        } reloc_lst;

struct syment {
        unsigned long   n_value =  0
        short           n_scnum =  0
        char            n_sclass = C_EXT
        } syment_0
```

The symbol table entry identifies the symbolic reference as external, C_EXT. It is a reference (or more generally, a symbolic declaration) because n_scnum is zero. The symbol me, in file foo1, is defined in source file foo2.

The definition of me in foo2 results in the following COFF entries:

```
address     opcode        source              comments
-------     ------        ------              --------
                          .file  foo2
                          .globl me           # external definition

                          .text               # start text section
0000    020000000040      me: add  number, r0 # opcode = 0200
                              .
                              .
                          ret

struct syment {
        unsigned long   n_value =  0
        short           n_scnum =  1
        char            n_sclass = C_EXT
        } syment_0
```

The .globl assembler directive is used for both declaration and definition. In foo1, .globl me is treated as a declaration since the me routine is not defined. In foo2, the .globl me is treated as a definition: the entry point to the me routine is clearly present. In foo1, the n_scnum value for the me symbol table entry is zero indicating no definition; on the other hand, foo2 has a symbol table entry for me with n_scnum set to one, the section it is defined in, text. The n_value is interpreted in this case as the relocatable address of me, and in this simple example is 0 since me is the beginning of text.

Keep in mind the important distinction between the symbol table entry for a definition where n_scnum is greater than 0; and for a declaration where n_scnum equals 0. These values play an important role in how the linker processes C_EXT symbol table entries.

Symbol Table Processing

The resolution process involves processing external symbolic references (declarations) and symbolic definitions.

To process (resolve) external symbolic references, the linker builds a **symbol table** list of all C_EXT **declarations** (external symbolic references) and C_EXT **definitions** (symbolic definitions) for all input object files. This symbol table list represents the symbols that need resolution and provide definition. Resolution occurs when the _n_name field of symbol table entry with n_scnum = 0 is matched with the same _n_name for a symbol table entry with n_scnum greater than 0. Symbols are matched by name (and both must be of storage class C_EXT). Once a symbol is resolved, the symbol table entry due to reference is discarded, and the relocation entries r_symndx updated to point to the symbol table entry containing the symbol's definition. The defining symbol table entry has an n_value that represents the symbol's relocatable address; therefore, relocation can now be performed on the external symbolic reference. The defining symbol table entry has the correct relocatable address because of the way the linker processes sections. See Figure 5-1.

Section Processing

Section processing includes relocation updating of the n_value field for the appropriate symbol table entries. Once updated, these symbol table entries become part of the symbol table of the output file. The processed symbol table entries have the following properties:

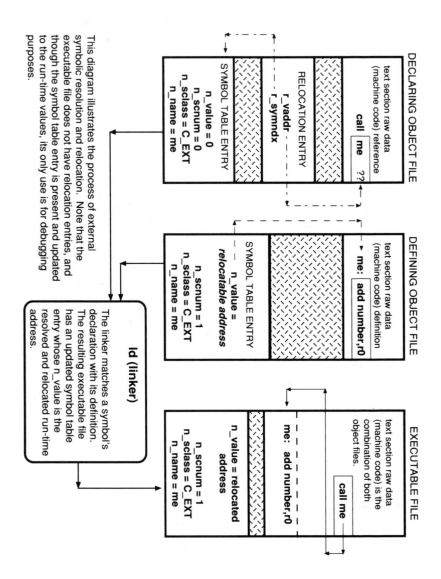

Figure 5-1. External symbol resolution and relocation

- The n_value is the relocated address. For example, when foo2 is being processed, its text section starts at a value that is a function of the previous section's text sizes. Therefore, the n_value for me must be updated accordingly (in general, n_value = n_value + sec_start_addr) since its object file n_value is 0. The output file symbol table entries contain n_values that are used to perform relocation.

- The n_scnum value is updated if needed. The n_scnum value always identifies the section where the symbol is defined. If the section number of text in the output file differs from the text section number where me is defined in its object file, the n_scnum is updated.

Generalized Linker Pseudo-Code

The processing of symbol table information on a per-section basis, and the maintenance of a current symbol table for symbolic references, makes implementation of external symbolic resolution relatively simple. The resulting code is general—it can relocate either local or external references.

Adding two additional steps to the basic relocation-processing sequence described in the Section "Multiple File Relocation—Local Reference," results in code that can perform external symbolic resolution:

- Once the section symbol table entries are processed (relocation information updated), check if any C_EXT definitions of the current section match names with any of the symbols in the symbol table. (Remember, the symbol table contains those symbols that require resolution). If there is a match, perform relocation, and discard both the relocation entry and the symbol table entry associated with the declaration (n_scnum = 0).

- If all sections have been processed, and there are still entries in the symbol table, then issue an error message for the **undefined symbols**.

The external-symbol resolution process is reflected by the following symbol-processing additions to the linker pseudo-code:

```
run_time_sec_addr = 0x100;                              /* step 1 */
for ( n=1; n==NUMBER_OF_OBJECT_FILES ) {
    init_object_file_vars ( n );

    for ( j=0; j==s_nreloc ) {
        reloc_addr        = get_reloc_addr( r_vaddr );   /* step 2 */
        sec_addr          = get_sec_addr( r_symndx );    /* step 3 */
        reloc_addr        = reloc_addr - sec_addr;       /* step 4 */
        reloc_addr        = reloc_addr + run_time_sec_addr; /*   5 */
        patch_reloc_addr  ( r_vaddr, reloc_addr );       /* step 6 */
        }

    run_time_sec_addr = run_time_sec_addr + s_size;      /* step 7 */

    /* symbol processing */
    relocate_n_value;
    add_C_EXT_defined_to_symbol_table_list;
    add_C_EXT_declared_to_symbol_table_list;
    match_and_relocate( symbol_table_list );
    }
```

The `relocate_n_value` function is the explicit statement to perform symbol table entry updating. This includes updating the
`n_value` to reflect relative changes in section start addresses, and
updating the `n_scnum` value. This function is, of course, performed
only on `C_EXT` definition entries.

The `add_C_EXT_defined_to_symbol_table_list` is used
with the statement, `match_and_relocate`. If a `C_EXT` defined
symbol table entry has the same name as an entry in the linker symbol
table, the symbol is resolved. Relocation can be completed, the relocation entry discarded, and the symbol table entry for the declaration can
be removed from the linker's symbol table.

The `add_C_EXT_declared_to_symbol_table_list` is also
used with the statement, `match_and_relocate`. This adds the
current section's symbolic references to the symbol table list. The
`match_and_relocate` statement then can look for symbols that
might define references from the current section.

Linking is successful if all sections (from all input object files) have
been processed and the symbol table is empty (no `C_EXT` declarations).
An empty symbol table means all references have been matched with
their definitions.

The linker's processing of library archive files is somewhat different from its processing of object files. Whereas object files can have cross references, library files cannot. This means that the position of the library file on the linker invocation line is important. For efficiency, a library file is scanned only once at the point where it is encountered. (The special linker-archiver interface that implements efficient library scanning is described in Chapter 6.) This means that a reference to a symbol that is defined in the library must be in the linker's symbol table at the point when it processes the library. The linker does not keep a list of C_EXT symbols defined in the library. Therefore, an object file must precede the library file on the linker invocation line so that the object file's symbolic reference is in the linker's symbol table when the library is scanned in search of symbolic definitions.

Linker Input File Order

The generalized linker pseudo-code explains why object file order is irrelevant when the linker is invoked. A symbol's reference in one object file can precede its definition in another object file. For example:

```
ld foo1 foo2 -o foo
```

Since foo1 appears before foo2, foo1 is processed first. This means that the external symbolic reference to me is placed into the linker's symbol table. When foo2 is processed, the linker checks the symbol table for matches against the current symbols defined in foo2. Since me is defined in foo2, there is a match; the symbol is resolved, and relocation completed.

Now consider the reverse situation:

```
ld foo2 foo1 -o foo
```

foo2 defines the symbol me. The symbol table entry is updated (relocated), and the entry is added to the linker's symbol table as a symbol that provides definition. Now when foo1 is processed, it results in a linker symbol table entry that references me, and there is an entry in the symbol table list that provides resolution: the symbol table entry for me's definition. As you can see, keeping track of both C_EXT references and definitions allows not only processing-sequence independence, but more importantly, object file cross dependence. (foo1 can define some symbols that are used by foo2 and reference symbols in foo2; foo2 can define symbols for foo1 and reference some symbols in foo1.)

Relocation Process Summary

Keep in mind the following important points about the description of the relocation process:

- The section-processing examples are generic. They are applicable to either text or data sections.

- The external symbolic reference example uses a reference to a subroutine entry point. The handling of an external symbolic reference to data is exactly analogous if the machine's architecture uses the same addressing modes in both cases (as the example CPU does). If addressing modes are different, the r_type field in the relocation structure tells the linker how to calculate the address.

- The examples demonstrating the process of relocation use a text section's relocation entry for a reference to a data section. This is probably the most common case, but a data section can also have relocation information

Data Section Relocation

An example of a data section relocation entry is shown in the following code example:

```
address   opcode                source              comments
-------   ------                ------              --------
                                .globl me           # external declaration
                                .text               # start text section
0000   030000000000             call me             # opcode = 0300
0006   020000000040             add   number, r0    # opcode = 0200
000c   030000000020             call it             # opcode = 0300
                                      .
0020   020000000040      it:    add   number, r0    # routine it
                                      .             # defined here
                                ret                 # return
```

```
                      .data          # start data section
0040   00000004   number:  .double 4     # data definition
0044   00000020   it_addr: .double it    # it's address
```

Notice the final line in the example. The argument to the `.double` data initialization directive is the symbol `it`, the entry point of that routine. Notice the value to which `it_addr` is initialized. The value is the address of the routine `it`. Since the address of `it` changes when the file is linked; so the value at `it_addr` must change too. This is an example of relocation in the data section: the data section's raw data is modified by the linker to reflect the linked address of `it`. This is also an example of local symbol relocation, but me could just as easily be used as the argument to the `.double` data initialization directive.

Symbols defined in a text section are used as arguments to the data initialization directives to create tables of entry points. C language code that creates an array of pointers to functions uses this type of coding.

Data symbols can be used as arguments to the data initialization directives. Data symbols create a value that is a pointer to some other data. The point of this example is that in general COFF is symmetric and recursive, and therefore, quite flexible and powerful.

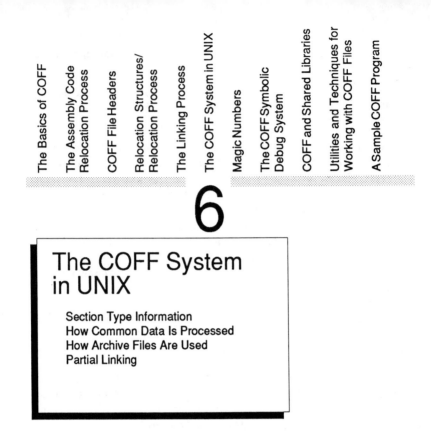

The Basics of COFF

The Assembly Code
Relocation Process

COFF File Headers

Relocation Structures/
Relocation Process

The Linking Process

The COFF System in UNIX

Magic Numbers

The COFF Symbolic
Debug System

COFF and Shared Libraries

Utilities and Techniques for
Working with COFF Files

A Sample COFF Program

6

The COFF System in UNIX

Section Type Information
How Common Data Is Processed
How Archive Files Are Used
Partial Linking

This chapter describes some of the important areas within UNIX where COFF is used.

The kernel loading mechanism and the linker use COFF information to properly handle and process COFF files. COFF information is also relevant to implementing and processing common data, archive files and their use, and implementing efficient partial linking.

Section Type Information

Section type information is used by both the kernel loading mechanism and the linker.

Section type information is contained in the last field in the section header structure, the **s_flags** field. The bits in this field represent two kinds of information:

- section handling
- section contents

A section's s_flags value can specify the type of section. The type of section determines how the linker and system loader handle the section. A section can only be of one type. If more than one type flag is set, either the linker, or the system loader at some point declare the file hopelessly corrupt and give up processing it.

A section's s_flags value can also identify the section's contents. Likewise, a section's contents can be of only one type (this is expected by most system loaders). The linker, in those few cases where it combines sections of different content (such as bss and data), always sets only one appropriate section type content flag. Section type mnemonics are explained in the next section.

Section Type Handling

Section type mnemonics and their values are defined in the same file as the section header structure, *scnhdr.h*. The following explanations use those mnemonics, but do not present the values since they differ widely from implementation to implementation. Also, there can be implementation-specific section types. The two places to find this system-dependent information is in the *scnhdr.h* file, and in your system-specific COFF Programmer's Guide.

The section type affects how the linker handles the section and the section's related information and contents. Based on section type, the linker determines whether the section requires allocation and relocation:

- Allocation deals with the application's memory space. If a section is **allocated,** that means it uses a part of the memory space available to the application; no other section can occupy this memory space. The linker output map shows the memory space occupied by the section.

- A section is **relocated** when the linker updates relevant addresses to reflect their final run-time values. This process involves updating relocation structures, symbol table structures, and where applicable, the pertinent areas of raw data.

Section type information is also used by the system loader. Depending on the section type, its raw data are either **loaded** into memory or **not loaded.**

Section Types

The following explanation is easier to understand if the following simplifying assumptions are made: 1) the two most significant bytes (MSB) of the s_flags field contain the section **contents** information, and 2) the two least significant bytes (LSB) contain the section **type** (handling) information.

The following types implement linker and kernel loader handling of sections:

STYP_REG

is the **regular section** type, and is the most common of all sections. It has a flag value of zero, and therefore is recognized when none of the other section type flags are set. For example, if the two LSBs of the s_flags field are zero, the section is regular and its contents determine handling. Regular sections always have one of the STYP content flags set. So, for a regular section, it's the **STYP content** flag that determines how a section is handled. The most universal **content** flags are:

STYP_TEXT   for a text section. Text sections are allocated, relocated, and loaded.

STYP_DATA   for a data section. Data sections are allocated, relocated, and loaded.

STYP_BSS   for a bss section. Bss sections are only allocated. They are not loaded because they do not have any raw data, and besides, bss sections are treated as data sections of all zero data when processed by the linker. Bss sections also are not relocated: they do not have relocation information. This is true by definition: relocation implies updating raw data to some run-time needed value, but bss does not have raw data. The bss section also does not have any line number information associated with it.

The respective bss section header fields, **s_scnptr** (section raw data file pointer), **s_relptr** (relocation information file pointer), **s_lnnoptr** (line number information file pointer), **s_nreloc** and **s_nlnno** (number of relocation and line number entries respectively), are all set to zero. Bss sections do have entries in the symbol table for symbols defined in the bss section.

STYP_INFO   identifies the comment section. The comment section does have raw data that typically is ASCII text. Needless to say, this section is not allocated, not relocated, and not loaded.

STYP_LIB   means that the section contains shared library information. This section is **relocated**, but not allocated nor loaded. Details are given in Chapter 9, *COFF and Shared Libraries*.

In addition to the regular section type, STYP_REG, the following two sections **types** are also common:

STYP_DSECT

is a dummy section type created by the assembler's **.dsect** directive. Dummy sections are used to create symbols whose values are used for relative addressing. How dummy sections are handled is implementation dependent. Some UNIX assemblers handle dummy sections internally, never creating a **STYP_DSECT** section type. Others do create the section, and it might include relocation information. In this case the section is **relocated**, but never allocated nor loaded.

STYP_PAD

section types are created by some linkers as a way of making two adjacent sections contiguous. This section is not relocated, not allocated, but is **loaded.**

The s_flags Field

The s_flags field controls the processing of sections. The s_flags-defined section processing can be summarized as follows:

```
/* is section type regular? */
if s_flags not in [ STYP_DSECT, STYP_PAD ]
    then  switch s_flags{              /* must be STYP_REG */
          STYP_TEXT : handle_text;    /* handling determined */
          STYP_DATA : handle_data;    /* by section contents */
          STYP_BSS  : handle_bss;}
          STYP_INFO : handle_info;}
          STYP_LIB  : handle_lib;}
    else  switch s_flags{              /* handle by type */
          STYP_DSECT: handle_dsect;
          STYP_PAD  : handle_pad;}
```

Note that each handle function has an implied break after it.

Combining Sections

As mentioned, a section can be of only one type (and this implies only one type of content). It is possible to use the linker to combine different types of sections. For some combinations this is perfectly valid. For example, combining a data section with a text section is OK. The section type is set to text, or in other words, data is interpreted as text. If execution goes to the data section, and there are valid machine instructions, everything is OK. But remember, data in a text section is write protected; it can't be modified.

Another allowable combination is bss and data. Bss sections are combined with data sections as part of the linker's normal processing of input object files. Bss sections become zero value data in the data section.

Other combinations are not allowed. Combining STYP_LIB with anything other than STYP_LIB is an error. Somewhere, at some point, something will complain.

As a general rule of thumb, STYP_REG contents can be mixed. Other combinations have no logical reason for mixing, and can produce either outright errors, or truly insidious software gremlins.

How Common Data Is Processed

Common data processing is a good example of how COFF implements a language specific requirement.

The .comm Assembler Directive

Common data is created by the **.comm** assembler directive and is contained in the bss section. The .comm directive has two arguments: the symbol's name, and its size in bytes.

Common data is most often associated with the FORTRAN language. (Some C compilers use common data for data that is external to functions. The new ANSI standard for C prohibits this, and common data will soon be the exclusive right of FORTRAN.) Common data in FORTRAN is used to multiply define arrays. This is the only instance where a symbol can be multiply defined. Arrays are multiply-defined in all source files that have to access the array, but the working size of the array is usually defined only in the main program source. Subroutines have a generic definition of the array, typically one element in size. The size of the array can be passed as a parameter to the subroutine, or the subroutine processing of the array can look for a tag end value.

.comm Symbols

.comm symbols create a symbol table entry of C_EXT storage class, an n_scnum equal to zero, and an n_value equal to the size of the definition.

There are two things to note here. First, though the .comm assembler directive is a symbol definition, the n_scnum is zero, indicating that the section number where the symbol is defined is unknown. And second, the n_value is not zero; it is the size in bytes as specified with a .comm assembler directive. The apparent contradiction in terms, n_scnum = 0 but the symbol being defined, is resolved when the processing of common data is considered.

Linker Processing of Common Data

A non-zero n_value with a zero n_scnum identifies a common definition. The linker collects common symbols of the same name, and then as a final phase of processing, sets the size of the symbol to the largest n_value found, and places the symbol into the bss section (where subsequent processing merges the bss section with the data section).

The linker chooses the best definition of the symbol: the one with the largest size can logically represent every instance of the symbol's definitions. In this way a subroutine can define an array to one element in size, but because of linking with the main program that contains the working size array, the subroutine ends up referencing the working sized array.

Multiple definitions for common work because the linker makes the decision of which definition to use. This is the only case where multiple defines are allowed. Multiply defined symbols of any other type (text, data, bss) are not allowed and cause a linker error condition.

How Archive Files Are Used

Archive files are handy collections of object files commonly called **libraries**. All archive library file names end with the **.a** suffix. Archive file is synonymous with library file; the two terms are used interchangeably.

The ar Utility

Archive libraries are created by the archive utility, *ar*. The object files in the archive file are called **members** of that archive file.

Not only can the *ar* utility create archive files, it can also perform a full range of library file maintenance such as:

- Deleting members.
- Replacing (updating) members.
- Extracting members.
- Listing the members.

The *ar* utility also has several more seldom-used functions such as a quick append of a new member.

Archive File Structure

The organization of the archive file is designed to implement an efficient interface with the linker. There is only one structure associated with archive files, and it is declared in the file *ar.h*. The archive structure has the following components:

```
#define ARMAG    "!<arch>\n"
#define SARMAG   8
#define ARFMAG   "`\n"

/* archive file member header is printable ASCII */
struct ar_hdr
{
    char   ar_name[16]; /* name is '/' terminated */
    char   ar_date[12]; /* date in decimal */
```

```
    char   ar_uid[6];     /* user id in decimal */
    char   ar_gid[6];     /* group id in decimal */
    char   ar_mode[8];    /* mode in octal */
    char   ar_size[10];   /* size in decimal */
    char   ar_fmag[2];    /* ARFMAG, the string to end header */
};
```

The header's information is in ASCII form. This is true of most UNIX implementations, though some declare the archive header contents as a mixture of long, short, and char.

The header's contents are in ASCII because one of the goals of the archive system is to provide a machine-independent file structure, and since char is really the only universal datum that does not vary from machine to machine, ASCII is used for the header's contents. The ASCII contents are easily converted to their corresponding numerical values by using the C library's *sscanf* function, which converts ASCII strings that represent either decimal or octal values.

Archive Header Fields

Archive header fields have the following uses and meanings:

ar_name   is the member's name. The name is terminated with a / slash, followed by spaces if needed to fill out the rest of the character array. Spaces are used to fill unused characters for all of the archive header's character fields.

ar_date   is the member's creation date as an ASCII string of decimal characters. After this string is converted to an integer value by sscanf, the integer value can be used as an argument to the *ctime* function which returns an ASCII string for the date. (The ctime function must be used since date is in the UNIX operating-system time format of number of seconds since 00:00:00 Greenwich Mean Time, Jan. 1, 1970.)

ar_uid   and ar_gid represent the file's user and group identification respectively. These fields have the same information as seen when doing a *ls –l* file listing, and if they are not null (set to all spaces) in the header, identify the original archive member creator's uid and gid.

ar_mode   is the permissions originally set on the member. This is
          the only field that represents an octal value. The octal
          value is interpreted as the permission bit pattern reported
          by an *ls –l* file listing.

ar_size   is the size of the member. This decimal value is the size in
          bytes of the entire COFF object file (as opposed to only text
          and data). The size can be used to find the header of the
          next member.

ar_fmag   is the magic string that ends the header. This field contains
          the ARFMAG defined string ` \n (grave accent followed by
          a newline character).

Archive File Format

The archive file begins with the archive file magic string ARMAG.
Immediately following this string is the first archive member's header.
Immediately following the header is the member, the contents of a
COFF object file in its entirety.

The next member's header is either ar_size number of bytes distant
if the current member ends on an odd-byte boundary, or ar_size plus
one number of bytes distant if the current member ends on an even-byte
boundary. Member headers always start on an even-byte boundary. A
newline character is used for filling between an even-byte ending
member and the next header.

And so on, and on: member header is followed by the member, followed by the next member header, for as many members as contained
in the library.

Special Linker Interface Member

The special linker interface member is always the first one in the
archive file, immediately following the archive magic string. Library
access by the linker is made efficient by the use of this special interface
member.

The special member begins with the standard archive header and is
recognized by its zero length name (ar_name[0] == '/'). The
contents of this member provide the linker with the information it needs

to efficiently use the library. The contents present a list of all the global symbol names in the library. These are defining symbol names: they represent either the entry point for a routine or the location of global data. Each symbol name is associated with an offset that points to the member's header, where the symbol is defined. This localizes the information needed by the linker. By using the archive symbol list of the first member, the linker can quickly perform symbolic resolution and easily extract the member that defines the symbol. The alternative to this is to scan the symbol tables of each and every member as often as needed. The contents of the first member make this inefficient approach unnecessary. The special member is often referred to as the archive symbol list or archive symbol table. The *ar* utility creates and maintains the archive file symbol table.

Archive Symbol Table

The contents of the archive symbol table are machine-independent. The symbol offsets (and the entry for the number of symbols present) are four-byte machine-independent integer values. Two special routines are used to read and write these offset values: *sputl*, and *sgetl*. These routines are in *libld.a*, a library that has many useful functions for working with archive files.

The format of the symbol table is as follows (See Figure 6-1):

- The value in the first four bytes after the header is the number of symbols in the table.

- The number of symbols value is followed by a sequence of four-byte integer values, one for each symbol. Each value is mapped to its corresponding symbol name. For example, the first value is associated with the first symbol name. The value represents a file offset that points to the header of the member where the symbol is defined.

- The symbol names follow the end of the offset values. The symbol name is represented as a null terminated ASCII string. Since strings are null terminated there is no restriction on their length.

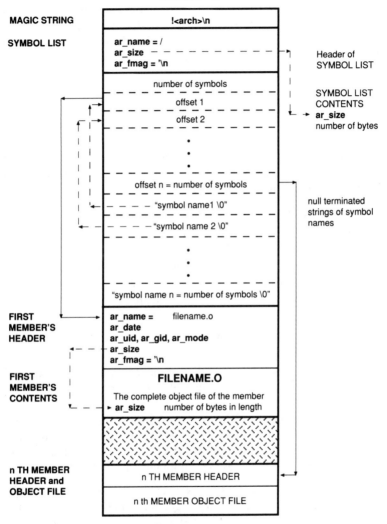

ARCHIVE FILE

Figure 6-1. The archive file structure

The point to note is that the symbol list offsets point to the header of the archive file member where the symbol is defined. This allows efficient searching of library files.

Handling and Accessing Archive Files

There's not much reason to develop special routines to handle archive files. The *ar* archive utility does practically everything that can be done to archive files, and the library *libld.a* has routines for accessing and manipulating COFF and archive files.

Partial Linking

Any time the linker processes an object file, it assumes that the resulting output file is executable. This means that that are no unresolved symbols, and that relocation information is discarded.

There are situations in which object files are linked but there are still unresolved symbols (or even if symbols are resolved), that the relocation information should be retained.

Such a situation is common when libraries are being developed. Suppose that a library is composed of several object files that have symbolic dependencies between them. There are two ways the library can be built:

- The library can be composed of several members: the individual object files.

- The library can be composed of one member: the object file that is the linked version of the individual object files.

The former way can be tricky. Positioning the archive members so that symbolic references precede the definitions can be especially frustrating since linkers don't always follow the same rules for resolving archive member external symbols as they do for normal input object files.

The second approach is the easier way to go. If you first link the object files to create one archive member, this way all of the symbolic dependencies between the library object files are resolved before they become a member of the archive. This approach is also much more efficient since presumably the library is to be used often, and it makes sense to do as much of the linking only once beforehand rather than every time the library is used.

Linker Retain Option

Object files that are linked to create an output file that is also an object file (not an executable file) must be linked with a special linker option. This is *–r*, the retain command line invocation option. This option tells the linker that there may be unresolved external references, and that relocation information (and symbolic information) should not be discarded. When this option is used, the resulting output file is suitable for subsequent input to the linker because all of the necessary relocation and symbol information is present.

Specifically, the linker does the following when invoked with the retain option:

- Does not complain about unresolved external references. Rather, unresolved reference relocation and symbolic information is part of the output file.

- Symbolic information that defines externals is present in the output file. Another object file with an external reference to a symbol defined in this file has all the information needed to resolve and relocate the reference.

The Basics of COFF

The Assembly Code
Relocation Process

COFF File Headers

Relocation Structures/
Relocation Process

The Linking Process

The COFF System in UNIX

Magic Numbers

The COFF Symbolic
Debug System

COFF and Shared Libraries

Utilities and Techniques for
Working with COFF Files

A Sample COFF Program

7

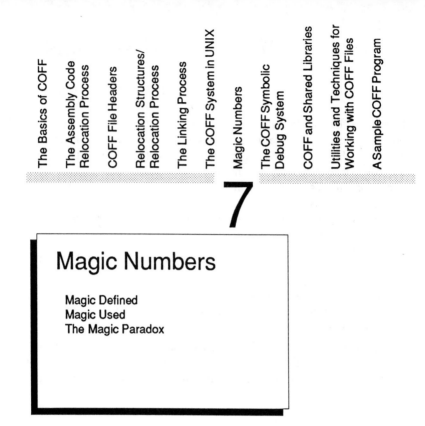

Magic Numbers

Magic Defined
Magic Used
The Magic Paradox

Magic numbers are one of the more romantic and mysterious topics within UNIX, but there really is nothing very magic or mysterious about them once they are understood. As a matter of fact, there is really so little to explaining magic numbers that this is the shortest chapter of the entire handbook.

Magic Defined

A number is magic because it contains so much information in so small a space. Period.

Magic Used

Magic numbers are used all over in UNIX. For example, the COFF file header magic number, f_magic, identifies the particular port of UNIX Anyone who pays upwards of $50,000 for the privilege of porting UNIX to their machine, receives their own unique f_magic number. The f_magic number is used by the system as a first check to insure that the file does come from a recognizable environment.

The optional header magic number, magic, identifies the run-time characteristics and structure of an executable COFF file (protections, section alignments). ARFMAG is a very good example of magic. ARF-MAG is the magic string that starts an archive file. If the first eight bytes of a file are ARFMAG, the probability is nil that the file is not an archive file. In all cases, the magic is that so much is deduced from so little.

If you're interested in becoming an expert on magic, a good place to start is with the file called *magic* in the /etc directory. This file has virtually all of the magic things found in UNIX. Another place to find some common f_magic numbers is in the file *filehdr.h*.

The Magic Paradox

The implementation of magic numbers does present an interesting, but purely speculative, paradox.

Magic numbers are defined as short values. Short values are two bytes long. A paradox occurs because to some machines the least significant byte (LSB) is in a lower, but contiguous, memory address than the most significant byte (MSB), while other machines interpret the value in the opposite fashion: MSB is the lower memory address, LSB is the higher memory address. This situation is also known as the byte flip-flop problem.

The paradox is designed into the COFF definition. Consider this scenario: you have a COFF file from an unknown environment, and you are aware of the byte flip-flop problem. This means that when you read the f_magic number, it might be reversed. So you look into some COFF documentation and find that the file header has a field (f_flags) that identifies the byte ordering used by the machine. Great you say, and proceed to read that field. This field has the octal value 01000 in it. Looking up the bit pattern, you discover that this pattern means:

This is a F_AR32W machine, MSB in low address.

Wonderful, your work is done! Well, not really, if you consider the situation carefully. This octal value can also mean relocation information stripped from the file if interpreted as LSB in low address. This is a possibility since an implementation might not set the byte ordering bits of the f_flags field. In other words, this system is not ambiguity free; the byte flip-flop problem should always be handled with care.

Though COFF is designed with the intention of being byte-order insensitive, in reality if you are dealing with a COFF file from an unknown environment, the byte flip_flop situation should be asserted from more than just the f_flags fields unless you can be certain that the f_flags do implement meaningful byte-ordering information. The new proposed ABI standard will probably go a long way in clearing up this somewhat nebulous area in COFF.

The Basics of COFF

The Assembly Code Relocation Process

COFF File Headers

Relocation Structures/ Relocation Process

The Linking Process

The COFF System in UNIX

Magic Numbers

The COFF Symbolic Debug System

COFF and Shared Libraries

Utilities and Techniques for Working with COFF Files

A Sample COFF Program

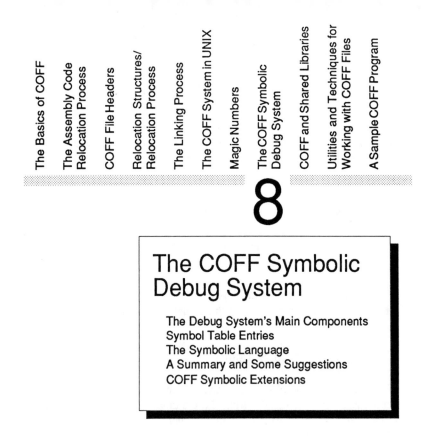

8

The COFF Symbolic Debug System

The Debug System's Main Components
Symbol Table Entries
The Symbolic Language
A Summary and Some Suggestions
COFF Symbolic Extensions

The COFF symbolic system is a uniformly portable debug system that quite adequately serves the needs of the C language, and in general is a good example of the COFF concept's portability and flexibility.

This chapter explains the details of the COFF symbolic system—from the individual entries in the symbol table to a discussion on expanding the system to accommodate other high-level languages.

The Debug System's Main Components

The three main components of the COFF symbolic debug system are the symbol table structure, line number information, and the string table. These three components make possible the basics of any state of the art debug environment:

* Source name symbolic reference to all program variables: from statics to automatics.

* Source line number reference for setting break-points, and source trace of program execution.

The COFF symbolic system has provisions for all of the information that goes into making a state of the art debug environment.

The Symbol Table Structure

The central portion of the debug system, the symbol table structure, has already been introduced during the explanation of the relocation process. In this sense, the symbol table structure plays a dual role: contributing vital information for relocation, and supporting symbolic debug. The symbol table structure can play this dual role because of two fields in it: the n_sclass storage class field, and the n_type symbol type field. Between these two fields, it is possible to characterize hundreds of high-level-language symbolic constructs, everything from the source file name to a variable on the stack (an automatic variable). The relocation process makes use of only a few storage class types, those that represent a relocatable address. (Most implementations have only four storage classes that represent relocatable addresses. Table 8-1 later in this chapter lists all of the common storage classes.)

The symbol table structure, syment, is declared in the file *syms.h*:

```
struct syment
{
  union
  {
    char    _n_name[SYMNMLEN];  /* symbol name, or */

        struct
        {
          long  _n_zeroes;    /* if _n_name[0-3] == 0 */
          long  _n_offset;    /* then _n_name[4-7] = offset */
        } _n_n;               /* (into string table) */

    char  *_n_nptr[2];        /* offset use declaration */
  } _n;
  long            n_value;    /* symbol's value */
  short           n_scnum;    /* section number */
  unsigned short  n_type;     /* type and derived type */
  char            n_sclass;   /* storage class */
  char            n_numaux;   /* number of aux. entries */
};

#define n_name    _n._n_name
#define n_nptr    _n._n_nptr[1]
#define n_zeroes  _n._n_n._n_zeroes
#define n_offset  _n._n_n._n_offset
```

Throughout this chapter's explanation of the COFF symbolic system, pay particular attention to how the n_value, n_scnum, n_type, and n_sclass fields are set and used. These fields, in a nutshell, are 90% of the COFF symbolic system.

Line Number Information

Line number information is a special part of the COFF file that contains line number structures. The line number structure associates every line in the source file that represents machine code with its relevant address in the text section. Line number structures allow creation of break-points by symbolic definition, and support source code trace of program execution. The section Line Numbers later in this chapter provides additional details.

The String Table

The string table is the final component of the symbolic system. Recall that the symbol table structure has a field of only eight bytes for the symbol name, but the C language supports symbol names of any length. If a symbol has more than eight characters, the name field in the symbol table structure does not contain the name, but instead is a pointer into the string table. The string table consists of null-terminated strings; therefore, it can support symbol names of any length. The section "Long Symbolic Names" later in this chapter provides additional details.

Symbol Table Entries

The central portion of the COFF symbolic system is the symbol table entry. The symbol table entries (the n_value, n_scnum, n_type, and n_sclass fields) can completely characterize the high-level-language (HLL) construction of the source program.

Symbol Table Entry Creation

A symbol table entry is created for every instance of a symbolic definition. When the symbol foo is defined in source, that is the point when a symbol table entry is created for it. A symbol table entry is also created for special symbols. For instance, a symbol table entry is created for the data section as a result of the .data assembler directive.

The symbol table entry for foo is for a user defined symbol. Of course, all user defined symbols get symbol table entries. After all, these are the variables of interest when the program is debugged. But in addition to user defined symbols, there also are special symbols that provide comprehensive information of the HLL construction of the source program. All special symbols begin with a period, just like the .data assembler directive. The data directive does more than create a symbol table entry, it also tells the assembler to start/continue a data section. The special symbol information directives, on the other hand, do nothing more than force an entry into the symbol table.

Assembler Symbol-Table Directives

Assembler symbol-table directives can describe every possible HLL construct. For example, the assembler directive pair .bf and .ef are used to designate the start and end, respectively, of a function definition. But of all of the dozen or so symbol-table assembler directives, the most important and frequently used is the .def and .endef symbol table assembler directive pair (.endef is .enddef in some implementations).

The .def assembler directive tells the assembler to create a symbol table entry for a specified symbol. Actually, the .def directive does more than just instruct the assembler to create a symbol table entry, for between .def and .endef, other assembler symbolic directives completely characterize the symbol table entry.

The name of the symbol follows the .def directive. After the symbol's name come directives that provide the contents for the n_value, n_sclass, and n_type fields of the symbol table entry. These are, respectively, the .val, .scl, and the .type assembler directives.

One example here is worth a thousand words. The following C program:

```
main()
{
int i=3;

        printf("%d",i);
}
```

has the following assembly source line for the symbol main:

```
.def _main; .val _main; .scl 2; .type 044; .endef
```

The _main symbol is the name of the C program's main() function. The .val directive has as its argument the symbol of the main function. This is because the n_value is the relocatable address of the main function (the symbol _main). The n_sclass field for this symbol table entry has the value 2 in it. This is a result of the `.scl` assembler directive. The `n_type` field has the octal value `044` as a result of the argument associated with the `.type` assembler directive. The `.endef` terminates the symbol `_main`'s specification. The semi-colons (;) are used to separate the directives.

In summary, the following assembler directives set the three most important fields in the symbol table entry:

- The **.val** directive specifies the **n_value** field.

- The **.scl** directive specifies the **n_sclass** field.

- The **.type** directive specifies the **n_type** field.

The Symbolic Debug Information Request

The symbolic debug information request must be made at compile time. This is because most of the symbolic information in a program comes from the specifications created within the `.def` assembler directive, and the `.def` directives are created by the compiler only when the source is compiled with the *–g* debug request command line option. As you can imagine, construction and interpretation of `.def` created information is of vital interest to compiler writers and debugger programmers.

Auxiliary Entries

Each symbol table entry can have one or more auxiliary entries. The number of auxiliary entries that a symbol table entry has is the value of the **n_numaux** field.

If a symbol table entry has auxiliary entries, they are contiguous with (immediately follow) the symbol table entry Auxiliary entries are the same number of bytes (usually 18) in length as the symbol table entry, but the structure of the auxiliary entry can be completely different from the structure of the symbol table entry. The structure of the auxiliary entry can serve implementation-specific needs such as expanding symbolic support for languages other than C. Also, as will be seen, the standard COFF symbolic definition makes use of auxiliary entries in several instances.

Since the auxiliary entry is the same size as the symbol table entry, it counts for one entry in the symbol table. But since auxiliary entries are always contiguous with their respective symbol table entry, this is transparent as far as access to symbol table entries is concerned. COFF structure pointers that point into the symbol table always point to a symbol table entry; never to an auxiliary entry.

Though auxiliary entries represent no problem as far as indexing into the symbol table, any updates (merges, deletions) from the symbol table must consider auxiliary entries.

Long Symbolic Names

The first eight bytes of the symbol table entry store information on the symbol's name.

The field for the symbol name is an overlay union of two structures:

```
union
{
  char  _n_name[SYMNMLEN]; /* symbol name, or */

      struct
      {
        long  _n_zeroes;   /* if _n_name[0-3] == 0 */
        long  _n_offset;   /* then _n_name[4-7] = offset */
      } _n_n;              /* (into string table) */

  char  *_n_nptr[2];       /* use for offset */
} _n;
```

Since the declaration is an overlay union, there are two ways to interpret the contents of symbol name (_n_name).

The interpretation starts by testing if _n_zeroes equal zero. If _n_zeroes is not zero, the first four bytes (_n_name) represent ASCII information: the name of the symbol. In this case the name must eight, or less, characters long. If the name is less than eight characters, the _n_name field is null-padded.

If the _n_zeroes field is equal to zero, the _n_offset field contains an offset into the string table. The string table is the final structure of the COFF file; it follows the symbol table. The string table consist of null-terminated character strings. Since the null termination is the only unique delimiter, strings of any length can be stored. The first four bytes of the string table represent a long value that specifies the number of bytes in the string table. An empty string table always has the the first four bytes for length, but the length value in this case is 0.

Long Symbol Name Access

Long symbol name access uses the _n_offset value. This offset value is relative to the start of the string table. But any access to the string table must compute the start of the string table by first considering the start of the symbol table plus the number of entries in the symbol table. This is because there is no explicit string table pointer. Even without an explicit string table pointer, the relevant information is found in the COFF file header. The start of the string table is easily found in a computation that uses the values from the following fields of the file header, *filehdr.h*, and the SYMESZ definition from *syms.h*:

```
strings = f_symptr + (f_nsyms * SYMESZ)
```

Because of padding within the symbol table entry structure, syment, the definition of the size, SYMESZ, from the *syms.h* file must be used instead of the sizeof(syment) function. See Figure 8-1.

Line Numbers

Line number information is created only when the source is compiled with the –g compiler invocation option that requests full debug information.

Though line number information is associated with the symbol table, the use of line number information is separate from most of the other symbolic information.

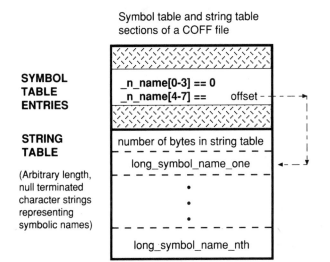

Symbol table and string table
sections of a COFF file

SYMBOL
TABLE
ENTRIES

_n_name[0-3] == 0
_n_name[4-7] ==   offset

STRING
TABLE

(Arbitrary length,
null terminated
character strings
representing
symbolic names)

number of bytes in string table

long_symbol_name_one

•
•
•

long_symbol_name_nth

If the first four characters of a symbol's name are null, the last four
characters represent an offset (relative to the start of the string table)
into the string table where the symbol's name is stored. Since the string
table entries are unstructured, symbols of any length can be stored.
Symbol names are terminated by a null character.

The first four bytes in the string table represent a long value that specifies
the number of bytes in the string table. An empty string table has a
length field, but the value stored there is 0.

Figure 8-1. Long symbol-name storage

Line Number Entry Creation

Line number entry creation occurs for every point in source that corresponds to a break point: a point where program execution can stop. This means that line number information is present only for the text section. That is all that is needed to implement symbolic or source line reference to execution points within the source code.

The Line Number Entry Structure

This structure is declared in file *linenum.h*, and looks like:

```
struct lineno
{
  union
  {
    long  l_symndx;  /* if l_lnno == 0 */
                     /*   then l_symndx */
    long  l_paddr;   /*   else l_paddr */
    } l_addr;
    unsigned short  l_lnno; /* line number */
}

#define LINENO  struct lineno
#define LINESZ  6  /* sizeof(LINENO) */
```

As you can see, the `lineno` structure has a union of two fields which means that there is a dual interpretation.

The interpretation works in the following way:

• If `l_lnno` is zero (valid line numbers start at 1), use the first definition of the first field, `l_symndx`.

• If `l_lnno` is greater than zero, use the second definition of the first field, `l_paddr`.

If the first field is interpreted as `l_symndx`, the symbol table entry is for the start of a function, and the `n_value` of the symbol table entry can be used as a break-point address. The only association between line number structures and the symbol table is for the entry point (starting point) of a function. This way, a break-point can be set at the start of the function by using the function's name.

If the first field is interpreted as a l_paddr, the value of l_paddr can be used as a break point. See Figure 8-2.

COFF line numbers

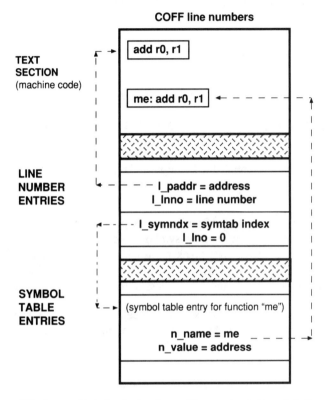

This diagram illustrates the two forms of line number entries. In both cases, the line number entry provides an address that can be used as a break point.

If l_lnno is greater than zero, the first field in the line number entry is interpreted as an address representing the first instruction for a line of source code.

If l_lnno is zero, the first field is interpreted as an index into the symbol table; in which case the n_value field of the symbol table entry is used as a break point address. This allows symbolic specification for break points.

Figure 8-2. Line number entries

Line Number Use

Line number use can be seen in *sdb*, the UNIX symbolic debugger. For example, *sdb* displays a program in the following way:

```
1:  main()
2:  {
3:      printf("%s","hello world\n");
4:  }
```

The numbers represent the source line numbers.

There are two ways to set a break-point at the beginning of the program.

The first way, you reference the function main() like so:

```
main:b
```

This instructs the debugger to put the break-point at the start of main. In this case the debugger uses the symbol table entry for main to get the break-point address. The break point address is the n_value of the symbol table entry for main. The n_value can be used because it a valid, fully relocated, run-time address of the function.

Or, on the other hand, you can specify a break-point for line 3, right at the printf statement. In this case the *sdb* command is:

```
3b
```

Since this is a direct line number reference, the l_paddr value is used as the break-point address.

This simple example illustrates how a debugger handles symbolic versus line number break-points. Keep in mind that in reality, debuggers like *sdb* are smart enough to figure out some subtle specifics.

For instance, setting a break-point at main results in *sdb* telling you where the break-point is actually set. In many implementations, *sdb* would say that the break-point is set at line 2. But you say there isn't anything at line two except a curly brace. Wrong. There may be function entry-point code which is not visible in the source listing. The program stops at line two, but automatic variables (the function's local variables that are defined on the stack) might not be valid. For example, the following `int` declaration is for a local variable:

```
1. bozo()
2. {
3. int i;
4. i = 5;
5. printf("%d", i);
6. }
```

`i` might not be valid at the line 2 break-point because, strictly speaking, the function has not yet been entered. Automatic variables are valid, or come into existence, only once the function is entered. The break-point at line 5, on the other hand, is definitely within the function, and the symbolic reference to any automatic variables is valid.

The important point about line number information is that it is fairly independent of the symbol table information with the exception of function entry or start points. This means the the implementation of line number debugging features has very little to do with the remaining COFF symbolic information that is presented regarding the specifics of storage class, types, etc.

The Symbolic Language

An individual symbol table entry is like a letter of the alphabet; therefore, a sequence of symbol table entries can spell out a word or even a complete phrase. The symbolic language, like any language, has rules that must be followed so that the resulting words and phrases are meaningful.

An individual symbol table entry completely specifies an individual quantum of debug information. But this debug information exists within the organized structure of a high-level-language (HLL). A HLL structure has scope rules for variables and **blocks** that represent a discrete quantum of activity. An example of a block is a for-loop. In the C language, the region of source enclosed by the { } curly brace pair represents a block. Scope rules for variables tell the debugger when a variable is accessible, or valid. For instance, automatics, the variables created for temporary storage once a function is entered, are valid only with the scope of that function.

Scope, block, and the entire hierarchy of the HLL structure are represented by the correct order of symbol table entries. For example, the .bf and .ef assembler directives enclose a definition of a function. Symbols within that function follow the.bf directive. And the definition of the function itself within the symbol table is determined by the function's definition in the source.

In the following elaboration of the COFF symbolic system, keep in mind that not only is the individual symbol table entry important, but so is the relative position of that entry within the symbol table. It is the order of symbol table entries that spells out the words that describe the HLL's construction. See Figure 8-3.

Storage Class and Type

The starting point for understanding the language of symbolics is the definition of two very important words that are used quite often:

- **Storage Class** (always refers to the **n_sclass** field)
- **Type** (always refers to the **n_type** field)

Storage class tells you how to interpret **n_value**. You have already been introduced to one storage class, C_EXT. A C_EXT storage class tells you that n_value is a relocatable address, but it doesn't tell what that relocatable address means to the program. After all, a relocatable address can be anything: a function entry point, an integer data address, a long data address, etc. This is where **type** comes into the picture. Type can be thought of as an adjective amplifier for storage class. Type tells you who, what, where, when, type of information. For C_EXT, type tells you what the relocatable address means to the program: is it an integer, function entry point, etc.?

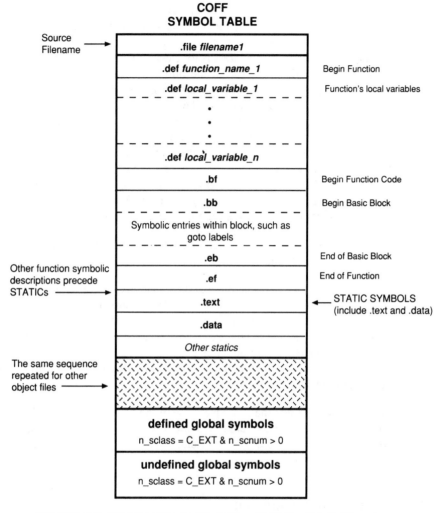

COFF
SYMBOL TABLE

Source Filename → .file *filename1*

.def *function_name_1* — Begin Function

.def *local_variable_1* — Function's local variables

•
•
•

.def *local_variable_n*

.bf — Begin Function Code

.bb — Begin Basic Block

Symbolic entries within block, such as goto labels

.eb — End of Basic Block

.ef — End of Function

Other function symbolic descriptions precede STATICs → .text ← STATIC SYMBOLS (include .text and .data)

.data

Other statics

The same sequence repeated for other object files →

defined global symbols
n_sclass = C_EXT & n_scnum > 0

undefined global symbols
n_sclass = C_EXT & n_scnum > 0

This diagram illustrates the order of entries in the symbol table. Note that the order is based on two levels. The first, represented by the .file entry, is at the source file level. The second, represented by such entries as .bf and .bb, is at the structural level of the particular source file. The final entries, the globals, are common to all source files. (Auxiliary entries are not shown.) Also, .bb - .eb are used only for basic blocks and are not present if a function does not have basic blocks.)

Figure 8-3. Symbol table order

If full debug information is not present (it will be present only due to a
–*g* compile), the type is 0 (null type). This is because storage class
information alone is sufficient for other uses than debugging, such as
the relocation process of linking. During the relocation process, it does
not matter whether that the address is for a char, function entry point, or
anything else for that matter. All the information that the relocation
process needs regarding the address is part of the relocation structure
(specifically the r_type field). On the other hand, it should be obvious that a debugger needs to know what a particular address is. For
example, whether an address is a char or an int determines how many
bytes constitute its length. A char is always one byte; int can be either
2 or 4 bytes. Type information, because of its role as an adjective for
storage class, does not play a major role in the dynamics of the debug
system as explained in the following sections. For this reason, the
complete discussion of type is left until near the end of this chapter.

The complete symbolic language dialect is declared in the files
storeclass.h, *a.out.h*, and *syms.h*.

The remainder of the explanation uses the mnemonics declared in these
files. Unless absolutely relevant to the COFF symbolic concept, the
values of the mnemonics are not presented. The values are available in
the mentioned files, and if you are curious you can peruse the files on
your system. In reality, no one uses explicit values when doing COFF
symbolic work, and to include them here detracts from the conceptual
structure of the symbolic system.

Also keep in mind that the subsequent use of the word value means the
contents of the n_value field of a symbol table entry. And likewise,
the word type refers to the n_type field, and storage class refers to the
n_sclass field.

Storage Class Interpretation

Storage class (n_sclass) tells you how to interpret *value*
(n_value) of the symbol table entry. The interpretation gets some
help from the section number (n_scnum) field.

You have already seen one instance of special interpretation of value based on section number. This was the case where section number is 0 (undefined external symbol) and value is greater than 0. Normally a section number 0 also has a value of 0. This represents a bss section symbol. On the other hand, a symbol declared by .comm (common symbol) has a non-zero value that represents the size of the common area. During linking, the linker collects like named common areas, and allocates the largest size to the symbol. This way all references to the symbol are safe since the largest size is used.

In all, section number (n_scnum) can determine four different interpretations of value. Two have already been presented: 0 means undefined external symbol, and a positive value represents the section number where the symbol is defined.

Section Numbers

Section numbers have the following definitions and meanings:

N_DEBUG   is –2, and means that value is for a special symbolic debugging symbol (an assembler symbolic directive).

N_ABS   is –1 and means that value is an absolute value.

N_UNDEF   is 0 and means the symbol is an undefined external symbol.

N_SCNUM   mnemonically means that value is a positive integer representing the section number where the symbol is defined.

N_ABS in general means value is not a relocatable address. For example, the storage class C_REG means that the symbol is a register. Value in this case specifies a particular register. If the symbol bozo was defined as a register type, when you ask the debugger to display the value of bozo, the debugger determines which register is bozo by looking at value.

N_DEBUG in general means that value has no meaning. In this case value is set to zero. N_DEBUG specifies special symbol table entries for tagnames. An example of a tagname in the C language is the symbolic declaration name of a structure:

```
struct foo_stuff {
                int x:
                } foo_1;
```

In the example, `foo_stuff` is the symbolic declaration of the structure. The symbol table entries for `foo_stuff` specify and describe the structure. `foo_stuff` is the structure's tagname. `foo_1` is the symbolic definition of a variable that is a `foo_stuff` structure; its symbol table entry uses (specifically references) the tagname. How this works to support debug is explained shortly, but for now the important point is that tagnames represent symbolic declarations that are associated with variables. In other words, a variable can have a tagname-specified form. Some other examples of tagnames in the C language include the typedef statement and array variables. For other languages, tagnames are also used for enumerations and sets.

Storage Class and Section Number Relationships

Storage class interpretation depends on both the `n_sclass` field, and the `n_scnum` field. Table 8-1 lists all storage classes, their valid section numbers, and the appropriate interpretation of the `n_value` field.

Table 8-1: Storage Classes

Storage Class	Section Numbers	Value Interpretation
C_EXT	N_ABS N_UNDEF N_SCNUM	External symbol relocatable address.
C_AUTO	N_ABS	Automatic (stack) variable. Specifies stack (frame) offset.
C_REG	N_ABS	Register variable. Specifies a register number.
C_LABEL	N_UNDEF N_SCNUM	Go to label's relocatable address.
C_MOS	N_ABS	Specifies *n*th member of structure.
C_ARG	N_ABS	Specifies *n*th function argument.
C_STRTAG	N_DEBUG	Structure tagname entry.

Storage Class	Section Numbers	Value Interpretation
C_MOU	N_ABS	Specifies *n*th member of union.
C_UNTAG	N_DEBUG	Union tagname entry.
C_TPDEF	N_DEBUG	Type definition entry.
C_ENTAG	N_DEBUG	Enumeration tagname entry.
C_MOE	N_ABS	Specifies *n*th member of enumeration.
C_REGPARM	N_ABS	Register parameter. Specifies register number.
C_FIELD	N_ABS	Specifies *n*th bit in a bit field.
C_BLOCK	N_SCNUM	Relocatable address for either the beginning of a block (.bb), or end of a block (.eb).
C_FCN	N_SCNUM	Relocatable address for either the beginning of a function (.bf), or end of a function (.ef).
C_EOS	N_ABS	End of structure entry.
C_FILE	N_DEBUG	Symbol table index.

The storage classes presented in Table 8-1 represent the more common and universal storage classes. Different implementations of UNIX operating-systems may use all, some, or even add to the list.

For example, recall the symbolic debug session where a break-point could be set at a line with only a curly brace ({). This point could be represented by a special storage class, C_BFCN, function begin point, and likewise the exit could be a C_EFCN storage class.

A good example of a special storage class is C_ALIAS. This storage class is produced when an object file is processed by the *cprs* utility. The *cprs* utility economizes the size of the symbol table by eliminating duplicate tagname specifications. When tagname symbolic information has a duplicate specification, only one sequence of symbol table entries is required to support symbolic debug needs. Identical structure tagname item's aliases are created by *cprs* to point to only one sequence of symbol table entries for the structure's specification. *cprs* is a useful utility for large programs that consist of many, many source files that have redundant inclusions of header files. *cprs* eliminates the duplicate tagname symbol table entries that result from redundant use of header files that declare structures. See Figure 8-4.

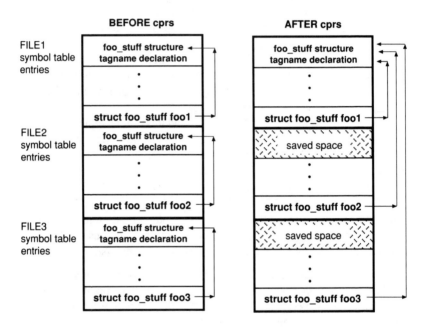

BEFORE cprs — **AFTER cprs**

This diagram illustrates how cprs saves space in the symbol table.

Duplicate tagname declarations occur when several source files use the same header file where the structure is declared. cprs consolidates all structure variable references to a single structure tagname declaration. This results in saving space and enhances the efficiency of the debugging process. (Of course, the consolidation is carried out for structures of the same type.)

Figure 8-4. cprs utility effects

As can be seen from the table, some n_value interpretations depend on the section number. For example, C_EXT is a relocatable address if section number is N_SCNUM, the section where the C_EXT symbol is defined. As mentioned before, a C_EXT with N_UNDEF section number is an undefined external symbol reference, and value is zero for .bss declared symbols, while for .comm declared symbols, value represents the size required by the symbol. C_EXT is really the only special case that is this complicated.

Other interpretations of value are quite obvious from the storage class alone. For instance C_AUTO, automatic (stack) variables is N_ABS meaning that value represents a stack offset value. Or C_REG is also N_ABS; its value specifies a particular register.

C_BLOCK and C_FCN are N_SCNUM, the section number where the symbol is defined. C_BLOCK and C_FCN storage classes are associated with the .bb and bf assembler directives that start a block and function specification, respectively. The n_value for both of these storage classes is quite naturally the relocatable address: the start/end address of the block, and the start/end address of the function, respectively.

C_STRTAG, C_UNTAG, C_TPDEF, and C_ENTAG are examples of N_DEBUG. N_DEBUG section number means the value usually has no meaning; instead, symbol table entries of this storage class represent special debug information.

C_FILE has a special interpretation for n_value and is an example of a N_DEBUG type where n_value does have meaning. C_FILE storage class value is an index to the symbol table. This is part of the information of the symbol table entries that map the complete structure of a high-level-language source file. More on this in the next section.

Symbol-table Entry Sequence

The sequence of symbol table entries maps the structure of a high-level-language (HLL) source. This sections details how the individual symbol table entries work together to define the complex structure of HLL program.

Assembler Directive Order

Assembler directive order is responsible for creating the correct basic sequence of symbol table entries. The symbol table has the following basic sequence (see Figure 8-3):

- The first symbol table entry specifies the filename. The .file assembler directive produces this symbol table entry.

- Subsequent entries are for functions. A function symbol table entry sequence starts with the .bf assembler directive followed by the .def assembler directive that specifies the variables local to the function. There are as many .def entries as there are symbolic variables in the function. The function symbol table sequence can also include basic block symbol table entries (the .bb, .eb assembler directive pair). The function symbol table entry sequence is terminated by the .ef assembler directive.

- Static symbol table entries follow the function symbol table entries. Statics include symbol table entries for the .text, .data, and .bss assembler directives.

- If the COFF file is executable, the filename-function-static symbol table sequence is repeated for every source file that was compiled with full debug information.

- Defined global symbol table entries follow the static symbol table entries of the last filename-function-static symbol table sequence.

- Undefined global symbol are the last entries in the symbol table. This is true only for an object file: an executable file does not have any undefined references. It wouldn't be executable if it did.

An extremely simple C program can demonstrate the basic symbol table structure.

The following C program:

```
int i=0;

main(j)
int j;
{
int k;
printf();
}
```

results in the following sequence of assembler directives that create the symbol table:

```
.file  "xxx.c"
.def    _i;   .val    _i;   .scl    2;  .type   04;  .endef
.text
.def  _main;  .val  _main;  .scl    2;  .type  044;  .endef
.def    .bf;  .val     .;   .scl  101;  .line    5;  .endef
.def    _j;   .val     8;   .scl    9;  .type   04;  .endef
.def    _k;   .val    -4;   .scl    1;  .type   04;  .endef
.def    .ef;  .val     .;   .scl  101;  .line    4;  .endef
.def  _main;  .scl    -1;   .endef
```

These directives are produced at the point where the symbols appear in the source. The actual machine code and data is not shown, nor are the **.ln** line number directives. The .ln directives are generated after every line that can be used as a break-point. For example, there is a .ln generated after the machine code that performs the call to the printf routine.

The only special point to note before examining the symbol table entries is the second instance of .def _main. This second instance has a storage class of –1. This usually means C_EFCN—physical end of function, and usually tells the assembler that the symbol table sequence for that function is over. No symbol table entry is created for the second .def _main. This is another example of the minor variations that can be expected between different implementations of COFF. Also note that the .val for .bf and .ef is a period (.). The period represents the current location counter, and codes as the relocatable address of the beginning and end of function, respectively.

Symbol Table Sequence Details

Symbol table sequence details reveal how the assembler directives map the structure of the HLL source. The resulting symbol table sequence for the previous section's example is:

index	_u_name	n_scnum	n_sclass	n_numaux
0	.file	N_DEBUG	C_FILE	1
1				
2	_main	N_SCNUM=1	C_EXT	1
3				
4	.bf	N_SCNUM=1	C_FCN	1
5				
6	_j	N_ABS	C_ARG	0
7	_k	N_ABS	C_AUTO	0
8	.ef	N_SCNUM=1	C_FCN	1
9				
10	.text	N_SCNUM=1	C_STAT	1
11				
12	.data	N_SCNUM=2	C_STAT	1
13				
14	.bss	N_SCNUM=3	C_STAT	1
15				
16	_i	N_SCNUM=2	C_EXT	0
17	_printf	N_UNDEF	C_EXT	

The explanation of the entries in terms of the sequence they must follow is:

- The first two entries, index 0 and 1, are the filename specification. The .file symbol table entry has an auxiliary entry (n_numaux = 1). The interpretation for all of the auxiliary entries is coming up soon.

- Index entries 2 through 9 are the main function symbol table entries. This includes entries for the beginning and end points (index entries 4 and 8, for .bf and .ef respectively), and for the function's local variables (index entries 6 an 7).

- Index entries 10 through 15 are for the static symbols.

- Index entry 16 is the defined globals (defined external symbols).

- Index entry 17 is the undefined globals (undefined external symbolic reference).

In addition to the sequence, note the storage class, section number, and value interpretation.

In particular:

- Index 0, for .file, is an N_DEBUG section number. Though in general N_DEBUG means value is meaningless, in the case of .file, the value has a very important meaning. Value is the symbol table index to the next .file symbol table entry. The .file symbol table value entries form a linked circular list (the final entry points back to the first) that is used by the debugger to quickly find the region of debug information associated with the particular .file *filename.*

- Index entry 6 is storage class C_ARG. This makes sense since the symbol it represents, j, is an argument to the function main. Since arguments are passed on the stack, value represents a stack offset, not a relocatable address. Therefore, section number is N_ABS.

- Index entry 7, for symbol k, is storage class C_AUTO because j is a temporary stack variable for the function main. Stack variables mean that value represents a stack offset, therefore the section number is N_ABS.

- The final two symbol table entries, index 16 and 17, are both C_EXT storage class. The section number makes the distinction between the defined C_EXT entry 16 for symbol i, and the undefined C_EXT entry 17 for symbol printf.

Auxiliary Symbol Table Entries

In general, auxiliary entries either implement a linked list structure within the symbol table that is used for efficient access of symbol table data by both the linker, the debugger, and related utilities like *cprs*, or contain debug/relocation information that is outside the scope of the symbol-table entry structure. Examples of auxiliary entries that contain special debug/relocation information are the entries for the .file, .text, .data, and .bss assembler directives.

The .file Auxiliary Entry

The `.file` auxiliary entry is the first auxiliary entry in the symbol table. The contents of this auxiliary entry are easy to explain: the entry contains a null-terminated ASCII string that is the filename. But, the exact implementation of this simple information is implementation-dependent. Some variations allow filenames no longer than 14 characters (System V allows 14 character filenames, so any source you want to debug can't be as verbosely named as the system allows). Other variations implement a scheme similar to the symbol name structure overlay that allows very long filenames to reside in the string table. (For instance, BSD UNIX system allows filenames up to 256 characters long.)

The .text, .data, and .bss Auxiliary Entries

The `.text`, `.data`, and `.bss` auxiliary entries contain the following information:

- The first four bytes (0-3) represent the section's length.

- The next two bytes (4-5) represent the number of relocation entries associated with the section.

- The next two bytes (6-7) represent the number of line entries for the section.

Note that not all UNIX operating system implementations make use of, or provide this information in the section's auxiliary symbol table entry. But the auxiliary entries that implement linked list structures are found in most implementations of UNIX operating system.

Linked List Auxiliary Entries

Linked list auxiliary entries are created for the following occasions:

tagname   declaration. A declaration of a structure results in that structure's tagname having a symbol table entry. The storage class for a structure tagname declaration is `C_STRTAG`. Unions and enumerations also have tagnames with storage class `C_UNTAG` and `C_ENTAG` respectively.

tagname	definition. Defining a structure (storage space allocated) results in a symbol table entry for the *tagname* structure type variable. The storage class in this case is either C_AUTO (on the stack), C_STAT (in a data or bss section).
.eos	is the symbol table entry for an end of structure. The storage class is C_EOS.
array	definitions with the storage class of C_AUTO and C_STAT.
.bb	the beginning of a block symbol table entry.
.bf	the beginning of a function symbol table entry.

Tagname Auxiliary Entries

Tagname auxiliary entries are used to implement a simple linked list structure. The following example is an instance of a tagname declaration and tagname definition.

```
struct foo1     /* tagname declaration */
    {
    int i;
    } fooi;     /* tagname definition */
```

This results in the following sequence of relevant assembler directives:

```
.def _foo1; .scl    10; .type 010; .size    4; .endef
.def     _i; .val    0; .scl    8; .type    04; .endef
.def .eos; .val     4; .scl 102; .tag  _foo1; .size 4; .endef
.def _fooi; .val _fooi; .scl    2; .type    010; .tag _foo1;
.size     4; .endef
```

The first thing to note is the way the first three .def assembler directives constitute the specification for the structure's declaration:

- The first .def is for the structure's tagname, foo1. The storage class (.scl) is a C_STRTAG, structure tag; the size represents the total size of the structure.

- The second .def is for the single field in this structure, the symbol i.

- The third .def is the end of structure, .eos. The storage class of 102 represents C_EOS. But the interesting entry here is the .tag assembler directive. The .tag directive tells the assembler to put the specified symbol into the tag field of the auxiliary entry associated with the symbol table entry for .eos. The use of this tag entry is explained later.

- The fourth and final .def is the symbol table entry for the definition of the variable fooi which is a fool structure. The .tag directive has the tagname of the structure's declaration, fool. The auxiliary entry's tag field is a symbol table index that points to the structure's declaration symbol table entry.

For example, the symbol table entries for this simple structure declaration look like this:

index	_u_name	n_scnum	n_sclass	n_numaux
0	.file	N_DEBUG	C_FILE	1
1	*filename*			
2	_fool	N_DEBUG=1	C_STRTAG	1
3				
4	_i	N_ABS	C_MOS	0
5	.eos	N_ABS	C_EOS	1
6				
7-12	(static	symbols	index)	
13	_fooi	N_UNDEF	C_EXT	1
14	**2**			

The symbol table entry that implements the linked list is entry 14, the auxiliary entry for the structure variable fooi. The 2 in the auxiliary entry points to the symbol table index for the declaration of the structure that constitutes the variable fooi. Symbol table index 2 is the tagname symbol table entry for the structure fool.

It should be quite obvious how this simple linked list provides vital debug information. The symbol table entry for the variable fooi does not have enough information to describe the fields in the structure. The fields are described in the symbol table entries associated with the symbol's tagname declaration: fool. So, when the debugger has to present information on the variable fooi, it uses the auxiliary entry to find the symbol table entries for the structure's complete specification. See Figure 8-5.

TAGNAME SYMBOL
TABLE ENTRIES

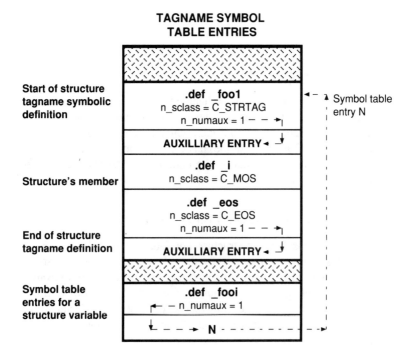

Start of structure
tagname symbolic
definition

Structure's member

End of structure
tagname definition

Symbol table
entries for a
structure variable

This diagram illustrates a structure type variable's relationship with its tagname symbol table entries. The symbol table auxiliary entry for a structure variable has an index value that points to the structure's tagname definition. The structure's tagname definition consists of a series of symbol table entries that completely characterize the structure.

Figure 8-5. Tagname entry schema

This is a good point to include the following minor detail. As you know, a structure variable can be defined without a tagname declaration: For example, the following code defines `fooi`, but without a declaration tagname:

```
struct            /* NO tagname declaration */
       {
       int i;
       } fooi; /* tagname definition */
```

The symbolic information is handled in exactly the manner just described, except that the compiler invents a tagname for the declaration. In that case, the symbol table entry for the tagname declaration (index number 2 in the example) has the the form: _.nfake_, where _n_ is a number sequence generated by the compiler for all instances where a **fake** tagname is needed.

Tagname Definition Auxiliary Structure

The declarations for this structure are found in the file _syms.h_. The structure's examples present only the relevant fields for the particular structure under discussion. The auxiliary entry declaration in _syms.h_ is a baroque declaration of structure unions and field overlays. But this does serve a useful purpose since that way one structure declaration can serve many needs, and access is efficient when implemented using switch statements.

The relevant fields in the auxiliary structure for a tagname definition are:

```
struct
{
    long x_tagndx; /* structure, union, or
                    * enumeration tag index */
    long x_size;   /* size of structure, union, or enum. */
}
```

The first four bytes of the auxiliary entry are for the linked list structure—the symbol table index to the relevant debug information.

No matter what the use of the auxiliary entry—from .eos to tagname—the first four bytes, x_tagndx are the linked list pointer. This is the value that is specified by the .tag assembler directive.

The tagname definition linked list is a trivial case—the index points to only one relevant entry—the symbol table entries that specify the structure (or union, or enumeration). This is the typical use of the x_tagndx field: to point to one entry that contains auxiliary debug information. This isn't much of a linked list, but it does serve a vital purpose.

The Tagname Declaration Linked List

This list is a true linked list in the sense that several structures are joined. The following code consists of two structure declarations that illustrates this list:

```
struct foo1 /* tagname declaration #1 */
     {
     int i;
     };

struct foo2 /* tagname declaration #2 */
     {
     int i;
     };
```

The symbol table entries have the following pointer relationships:

- The x_endndx field in the auxiliary entry associated with the tagname declaration of the symbol foo1 points to the next tagname declaration, the symbol table entry for foo2.

- The x_tagndx field in the auxiliary entry associated with the .eos of foo1 points to the symbol table entry for foo1.

- The x_endndx field in the auxiliary entry associated with the tagname declaration of the symbol foo2 points to the first entry of the statics, usually the symbol table entry for the .text section.

- The x_tagndx field in the auxiliary entry associated with the .eos of foo2 points to the symbol table entry for foo2.

The x_endndx field implements a true linked list of structure declarations. This linked list is used by the debugger, and other utilities that manage COFF files. For example, the *cprs* (compress) utility uses this structure to efficiently search out duplicate declarations. See Figure 8-6.

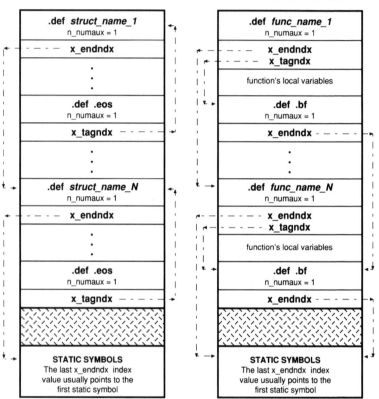

This diagram illustrates how auxiliary entries are used to implement linked lists of symbolic information. The left-hand diagram shows a structure linked list. The right-hand diagram shows a function linked list.

Figure 8-6. Auxiliary entry linked list structure

In general, the x_endndx field is used to implement a true linked list, whereas the x_tagndx field usually points to only one item that contains helpful, vital, auxiliary information.

Tagname Declaration Auxiliary Structure

The declarations for this structure are found in the file *syms.h*:

```
        /* Tagname declaration auxiliary entry format */
struct
{
    unsigned short  x_size;     /* size of structure,
                                 * union, or enum. */
    long int        x_endndx;   /* index to next structure,
                                 * union ... */
}

        /* auxiliary entry for .eos (end of structure) */
struct
{
    long int        x_tagndx;   /* index to structure's
                                 * name entry */
    unsigned short  x_size;     /* size of structure,
                                 * union, ... */
}
```

Function Auxiliary Entries

Function auxiliary entries implement a dual efficient list structure (which, by the way, is only partially implemented in most UNIX operating-system versions).

The auxiliary entry for the definition of a function has an x_tagndx and an x_endndx field. The complete symbol specification of a function consists of the following symbol table entries:

- A .def for the function name. This symbol table entry has the auxiliary entry that contains an x_tagndx field, and an x_endndx field.
- The .defs for local/stack variables, if any, are next.

- A .def with a **.bf** signifies the beginning of the function. The .bf symbol table entry has an auxiliary entry.

- A .def with an **.ef** signifies the end of the function. The .ef symbol table entry has an auxiliary entry.

The auxiliary entry for the function name uses the x_tagndx field to point to the function's .bf symbol table entry—which is rather vital, helpful, auxiliary information on the function. The x_endndx points to the next symbol table entry for a function name, or if the final entry, points to the first static symbol, usually the symbol table entry for .text. This is the typical linked-list use of the x_endndx field.

The auxiliary structure for the function name also has fields for the line number that is the start of the function, and the function's size.

The .bf auxiliary entry has a x_endndx field that points to the next function's .bf symbol table entry. The .bf auxiliary entry also has a line number field for the line of the function where code begins.

The .ef auxiliary entry has only one field, the line number associated with the end of the function.

The use of these lists is quite obvious. The linked list of function names makes rippling through only functions fast and efficient.

The .bf linked list is useful for rippling through only the code of the functions, and is fast and efficient access to function code line numbers.

The x_tagndx field allows one step access to the code of the function. If the x_tagndx field is used, there is no need to sequentially ripple through the local variable symbol table entries to get to the beginning of the function's symbol table entries that start with .bf.

As elegant as the function-related linked list structures are, the actual use falls short of the potential. UNIX operating-system implementations typically use only the x_endndx field of the function name auxiliary entry. The other fields are usually set to zero.

The Function Auxiliary Structure

The function auxiliary structure has the following declaration:

```
        /* function definition auxiliary entry */
struct
{
  long x_tagndx;  /* pointer to function's .bf */
  long x_fsize;   /* size of function */
  long x_lnnoptr; /* pointer to function line number entry */
  long x_endndx;  /* pointer to next function */
}

        /* .bf auxiliary entry */
struct
{
  unsigned short x_lnno;   /* start of code line number */
  long           x_endndx; /* pointer to next function's .bf */
}
        /* .ef auxiliary entry */
struct
{
  unsigned short x_lnno;   /* end of function line number */
}
```

Block and Array Auxiliary Entries

Block and array auxiliary entries are implemented in a manner analogous to the structure (tagname) and function auxiliary entries. Blocks are handled in much the same manner as structures, with the exception that the auxiliary entries are simpler, containing only a x_endndx linked list of blocks and line numbers associated with the beginning and end of a block. And though the array auxiliary entry has room for all kinds of information, usually only the size field is used.

Types

The variable type is specified in the symbol table entry's n_type field.

The n_type field's 16 bits are divided into six two-bit fields, and one four-bit field.

The Fundamental Type

The fundamental type is specified in the bit pattern in the 4-bit field. There are sixteen fundamental types (just the right size for the field). The fundamental types describe the **non-decomposable** data found in the C language. The following is a list of fundamental types along with their mnemonics from the file *syms.h*:

Table 8-2: Fundamental Types

Type	Meaning
T_CHAR	character
T_SHORT	short integer
T_INT	integer
T_LONG	long integer
T_FLOAT	floating point
T_DOUBLE	double word
T_STRUCT	structure
T_UNION	union
T_ENUM	enumeration
T_MOE	member of enumeration
T_UCHAR	unsigned character
T_USHORT	unsigned short
T_UINT	unsigned integer
T_ULONG	unsigned long

At first you may question that a fundamental type of, for instance, T_STRUCT can be decomposed to its fields. But if this is done, the structure loses its meaning—decomposition destroys information inherent to specifying a structure. This becomes clear once **derived types** are introduced.

There is also a T_NULL fundamental type. T_NULL is used where appropriate, such as the type for C_BLOCK or C_FCN where there can be no fundamental type, and if debug information is not requested at compile time, then all variables are typed T_NULL.

Derived Types

Derived types in conjunction with T_*types* can specify many high-level-language constructs. There are four derived types. Four is the most that can be represented in a two-bit field, but even so, all C language constructs can be represented:

Table 8-3: Derived Types

Type	Meaning
DT_NON	no derived type
DT_PTR	pointer
DT_FCN	function
DT_ARY	array

A Few Examples

A few examples show how fundamental type and derived type work to completely specify C language constructs. For example:

```
int *num();
```

This is a declaration for a function (num) that returns a pointer to an integer.

The fundamental type is T_INT, integer, since this is the object of the declaration. The first derived type field in n_type is DT_FCN, a function. The second derived type field in n_type is DT_PTR. The specification is complete. Notice that type can be decomposed without losing the information that is the object of the declaration: the fundamental type. Removing the function and pointer part still leave you with the object of the declaration, the int.

Another example:

```
char *ray[5][5][5];
```

Here the fundamental type is char. The first three derived type fields specify DT_ARY, array, while the final field completes the specification by adding DT_PTR. Notice the order of specification follows a least damage by decomposition sequence. Removing pointer from the declaration does less damage to the basic information than removing one of the indices to the array.

The symbol table entry's n_type field is specified by the .type assembler directive. And as seen, the .type assembler directive is part of the .def sequence of assembler directives that specify a symbol table entry.

The value for .type is often specified in octal format or with macros that perform shifting, and anding of the basic fields to construct the n_type field.

Type Macros and Defines

Type macros and defines can be found in the file *syms.h*. These macros and defines are useful for working with the contents of the n_type field. For example:

```
#define ISPTR(x) (((x) & N_TMASK) == (DT_PTR << N_BTSHFT))
```

This macro tests if a derived type field specifies a pointer.

This is all that there is to types. The only detail beyond this is storage class versus allowable types. Standard UNIX operating system COFF documentation has several tables that deal with this rather boring issue; for the most part, types and storage class associations are intuitively obvious.

A Summary and Some Suggestions

The COFF symbolic system is baroque and complicated, a real challenge to any disciplined mind. However, by observing the following suggestions you can establish a sound technique for investigating COFF symbolic dynamics:

- There is, for the most part, a one-to-one correspondence between assembler directives and symbol table entries. The best way to learn the symbolic system in detail is to utilize the –*S* flag of the compiler (and assembler) to create assembly source text files that can be studied.

- The examples presented in this chapter emphasize the generic concepts of the COFF symbolic system. You can expect to find deviations in your UNIX operating-system implementation. But, . . .

- You now know how to investigate any COFF symbolic issue:

  1. Write some pertinent C source code,
  2. Have the compiler create an assembly source file (*–S* flag), and
  3. Study the source with the knowledge of assembler directives and COFF symbolic structure you have gained from this chapter.

- Remember that the auxiliary entry structures presented in this chapter show only the relevant fields. In those cases where x_tagndx is not the first field, there is dummy spacing between the start of the structure and the first field.

COFF Symbolic Extensions

Though the COFF symbolic system has been designed to be portable, it is also the area that usually deviates most quickly from any notion of a standard UNIX operating-system environment. This is because the COFF symbolic system is often modified (extended) to adequately serve some other language, such as FORTRAN or Pascal, or is integrated with some high-powered proprietary debug system. The modifications are transparent to the user, but are of vital interest to compiler writers, assembler programmers, and debug specialists.

The COFF symbolic system is quite adequate for full symbolic debugging of C programs. But even with C programs, the limitations of the COFF symbolic system can become apparent for very rare situations. For example, a 6-dimensional array of pointers to characters cannot be represented as a type because this type representation requires one more derived type field than is available. As you can see though, that for C, this is not really a problem: 6-dimension arrays are not that common.

Though adequate for C, the type and the storage class COFF symbolic definitions are deficient in representing other languages, even the fairly symbolically undemanding FORTRAN language.

There is no easy solution to these deficiencies. The COFF C based symbolic definitions cannot simply map to other popular languages like Pascal. The solution is quite drastic and begins with a modification of the symbol table entry.

The Environment Field

The solution begins by adding a new field to the symbol table structure (Note: some implementations already have this field). This is the **n_env**, or **environment** field. This field contains a value that identifies the source language. This identification is important not only to the debugger, but also to the linker. In general, expanding COFF symbolics requires modification in four areas: compiler, assembler, linker, and debugger.

The compilers must specify the debugging environment. The assembler requires modification because new assembler directives must be added; among these is the compiler generated directive that specifies the environment. The linker, in a few cases, must understand new rules for building and ordering the symbol table. And lastly, the debugger puts all of these modifications to use by providing high-level debug features.

C Versus Pascal: Some Issues

As can be seen, extension of the COFF symbolic system is no small job. But it is a necessary job for symbolic debug of a language like Pascal. For example, consider just some of the deficiencies of the C based COFF symbolic system as it relates to Pascal:

1. Pascal allows nesting of procedures. The C COFF symbolics do not support nested procedures since there is no such thing in C. The modification to implement nested procedures is quite extensive. It requires the nesting .bf-.ef directive pair. This has a profound affect on the structure of the symbol table, and the way it must be interpreted by the debugger.

2. The C fundamental types represented in COFF are inadequate for Pascal. Pascal has boolean, cardinal, set, and file fundamental types. There are no analogs of these types in C.

3. Pascal (and other languages) support packed records. The C COFF symbolic system has no way of indicating a packed type.

4. Pascal array indices can range between any values. The C COFF symbolics assumes that an array index starts at 0. (This, by the way, is one of the few inadequacies of C COFF symbolics in relation to FORTRAN.)

5. Pascal languages often have a string type. This is unknown to the C COFF symbolic system.

In addition to these dominant Pascal requirements, two other deficiencies are often cited that also apply to the C language:

1. Current COFF symbolics do not support line numbers for included files.

2. The current symbolic debug system does not really implement any compatibility checking of the source file versus its object file. This is needed so that source level debug can identify an out-of-date object file.

A Modified Symbol Table Entry

The value of the environment field tells the linker and debugger the source language of the symbolic entries. Based on this value, proper interpretation of the type and storage class fields is made. Every language really needs its own types and storage class.

For example, a Pascal array symbol table entry might be defined in the following way:

```
.def _pray; .scl   P_ARRY;   .type PRY;      .size    40;
.tag     6; .range CHR,10,19; .range INT,1,30; .env PPP; .endef
```

Notice how this hypothetical symbol table entry is implemented. The .env directive set the environment field of the symbol table entry. This gives special meaning to the .scl and .type values. Lastly, note that this is a multidimensional array because two ranges are specified. The .range directive is also new and each range results in a auxiliary entry. The existence of the auxiliary entries makes possible virtually any expansion that might be imagined.

The Basics of COFF

The Assembly Code Relocation Process

COFF File Headers

Relocation Structures/ Relocation Process

The Linking Process

The COFF System in UNIX

Magic Numbers

The COFF Symbolic Debug System

COFF and Shared Libraries

Utilities and Techniques for Working with COFF Files

A Sample COFF Program

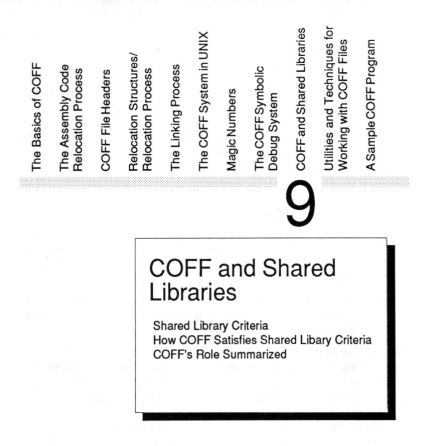

9

COFF and Shared Libraries

Shared Library Criteria
How COFF Satisfies Shared Libary Criteria
COFF's Role Summarized

Shared libraries are a good example of the flexibility inherent in the COFF definition.

Normal, relocatable libraries, such as *libc.a*, are part of the executable files that use them. Every executable file contains portions of (or in rare cases most of) *libc.a*. And since there are thousands of executable files at many UNIX operating system installations, this means there are just as many duplications of *libc.a*. Clearly, this is inefficient use of disk space.

Not only is this inefficient use of disk space, the use of normal libraries does not lend itself to performance tuning. If code that is used by many processes can be segregated to a particular area of memory, this reduces the paging (or swapping) of this code because it has a high hit ratio (since it is used by many processes). But performance tuning of this type is not possible with the normal libraries because the libraries are not within the same memory region on a per process basis.

If processes could **share** common code such as *libc.a*, the benefits are obvious: smaller executable files and improved system performance. And this is what shared libraries do.

Shared Library Criteria

In order to meet the desirable goals of smaller executable files and improved system performance, shared libraries must satisfy the following criteria:

1. A shared library must reserve for itself a region of memory. Though other processes can use this region, the possibility for true performance tuning does exist.

2. A shared library must consist of two components: the portion that is linked with object files during the creation of the executable file (this is called the **host library**), and the portion that actually contains the library's code (this is called the **target library**).

The host library contains only enough information to define the entry points to the library's functions. Therefore, linking with a host library reduces the size of the executable file.

The target library contains the machine code for the library's functions. The target library is managed by the kernel and is always loaded into a predetermined memory range. This technique results in a performance effective use of the library's code.

3. And lastly, and quite obviously, a shared library must be re-entrant. This, for the most part, is not at all a problem for shared libraries written in C.

These criteria for shared libraries are satisfied by COFF in a remarkably simple manner.

How COFF Satisfies Shared Library Criteria

The implementation of shared libraries in the UNIX operating system requires modification to the kernel loader and the linker, and the creation of special utilities. Modification of the kernel loader and linker is needed to satisfy the first and the last shared library criteria. COFF does its part by making possible the second shared library criteria: the existence of the **target** and the **host** libraries.

Consider how libraries in general become part of an executable file. The application makes a reference to some external symbol that is the entry point to a library routine. When the application's object file is linked, the linker performs relocation by providing the run-time address of the referenced library routine. So far this is true whether the library is shared or not. The difference begins when the linker tries to include the text section of the library file. For normal library files, the text section (code) of the referenced routine is included in the executable file. For shared libraries, the executable file does not include the text section of the referenced routine.

The .lib and .init Sections

The `.lib` and `.init` sections are created especially for the implementation of shared libraries.

Instead of text sections, the **target** shared library contains a special **.lib** section. The `.lib` section contains only relocation information: the addresses of the referenced routines. This works because the addresses of the referenced routines are static; they do not change once the shared library is designed and built. And this, of course, is possible because the shared library reserves a region of memory for itself.

NOTE

Strictly speaking, the host library can change without affecting routine addresses because all entry points are indirect: all routines are entered via a branch table. As long as the entry point to the branch table does not change, any other change to the library, such as a bug fix that alters the code, is transparent to an application that is linked with that shared library.

The target shared library also contains another special section. This is the .init section. The .init section is the only part of the shared library code that becomes part of the executable file. The .init section contains nothing more than a sequence of initialization statements. These initialization statements typically initialize pointers imported from the application. Because the .init section is machine code, the linker usually makes it part of the text section of an executable file.

The mkshlib Utility

The *mkshlib* utility builds shared libraries according to specified instructions (a script file) much in the same manner as *make*. The .lib section is created by the *mkshlib* utility.

The .section Assembler Directive

The .section assembler directive is used to create a section named .init with the attributes of a text section (machine code). This assembler directive is usually found only in one of the shared library C run-time start-up files (either *crt1.o* or *crtn.o*) where the initialization sequence is called as program execution starts.

COFF's Role Summarized

As can be seen, most of the burden of implementing shared libraries falls outside of COFF. COFF simply makes the integration of this rather major enhancement simple and elegant. All COFF has to do is allow the new special sections, lib and init, but it is up to the linker and system loader to handle them in accordance with shared library requirements. For example, when the linker sees a lib section, it performs only relocation and does not load the contents into the executable file. But the kernel loader function has an even greater responsibility. When an application that is linked with a shared library is loaded into memory, the kernel must determine if the library is already in memory or not.

Figure 9-1 shows how shared library applications map to memory at run-time.

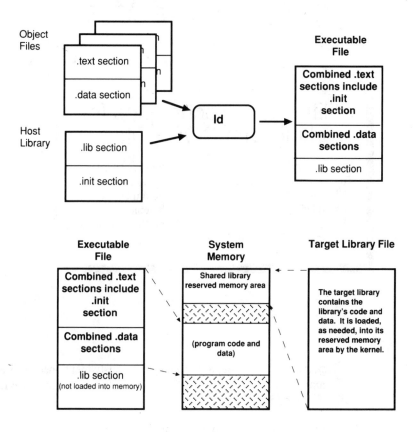

Figure 9-1. Shared library use

The Basics of COFF

The Assembly Code
Relocation Process

COFF File Headers

Relocation Structures/
Relocation Process

The Linking Process

The COFF System in UNIX

Magic Numbers

The COFF Symbolic
Debug System

COFF and Shared Libraries

Utilities and Techniques for
Working with COFF Files

A Sample COFF Program

10

Utilities and Techniques for Working with COFF Files

Using Header Files
The .ident Assembler Directive
The mcs Utility
The od Utility
The dump Utility
The .section Assembler Directive

The cprs Utility
The conv Utility
The nm Utility
The ctime Function
The COFF Library

The chapter contains a summary of many previously mentioned utilities that manipulate COFF files, and a few previously unmentioned trivial details of general interest.

The utilities summary and trivia information covers:

- Using COFF header files

- Assembler directives: .ident and .section

- *mcs*

- *libld.a*
- *od*
- *dump*
- *conv*
- *nm*
- *cprs*

Note that not all of these utilities are found in all System V implementations. For instance, *mcs*, *conv*, *cprs*, and the listed assembler directives are typically associated only with System V.3.

Using Header Files

The COFF related header files provide much more than just useful defines and macros. The header files in general should be examined for the following two special reasons:

1. The header file might contain an explicit define of a structure's size. If it does, use that size instead of the `sizeof()` function.

2. The header files declare the COFF structures in as portable way as possible. This means that 32-bit values are consistently declared as long values.

Always check the header file declared structure for the proper typing whenever a field from that structure is explicitly defined outside that structure.

By following these two simple suggestions, your code should be portable, and time-wasting debug is minimized.

The .ident Assembler Directive

The **.ident** assembler directive is responsible for creating comment sections in the COFF file. The argument to the `.ident` directive is an ASCII string which is concatenated to the COFF file's comment section. The string can consist of any useful, or not so useful, comment.

The mcs Utility

The *mcs* utility is used to manipulate comment sections. For instance, the *mcs* utility can be used to remove not so useful comments, or simply display the comments for everyone's amusement.

Remember, whatever the `.ident` assembler directive can put in, mcs can take out.

The *mcs* utility is usua.ally cataloged under *mcs*(1) in the *User's Reference Manual*.

The od Utility

The *od* utility is an octal dump utility. The *od* utility performs unintelligent raw dumps of a file's contents. Any number of bases for the output can be selected. Perhaps the *od* utility's most useful option is the offset option. The offset option specifies the starting point of the dump, and can be used to experiment with file pointer values.

The *od* utility is usually cataloged under *od*(1) in the *User's Reference Manual*.

The dump Utility

The *dump* utility is specifically designed to output selected portions of a COFF file: object, executable, and archive.

The *dump* utility has numerous options to specify a particular section of a COFF file and the format of the output.

The *dump* utility is usually cataloged under *dump*(1) in the *User's Reference Manual*.

The .section Assembler Directive

The assembler's **.section** directive was created in response to the need of a special section for shared libraries. The .section allows the specification of a section name, and usually the section content's type.

Currently, the use of the .section directive is very rare; it's used only in one of the shared library C run-time start-up files (usually *crtn.s*, the source to *crtn.o*) to create the .init section. The .init section contains shared library initialization code.

Though the use of the .section directive is at the moment limited, its main purpose is to allow easy creation of special COFF sections that might be needed in the future.

The cprs Utility

The *cprs* utility is used to save space in object files. This utility eliminates duplicate tagname entries in the symbol table. The amount of space saved can be considerable for applications that have redundant header file includes that have redundant structure declarations.

The *cprs* utility is usually cataloged under *cprs*(1) in the *User's Reference Manual*.

The conv Utility

The *conv* utility is one of the first steps in the development of a host-independent object file format. This utility performs object file conversions. The conversion performed depends on the specified options, but usually involves changing byte order. Typically, the *conv* utility is used only on archive files.

The *conv* utility is usually cataloged under *conv*(1) in the *User's Reference Manual*.

Also, see the *convert* utility. It is usually cataloged under *convert*(1) in the *User's Reference Manual*.

The nm Utility

The *nm* utility is an invaluable tool for exploring program symbols. The *nm* utility provides comprehensive symbol table information on either object, or archive files.

The *nm* utility is often used to find the definition point of a symbol. *nm* options such as sorting the output by symbol name help in efficiently pinpointing the symbol of interest. And, of course, the output of *nm* can be piped to a utility like *grep* that can filter out unwanted symbol names.

The *nm* utility is usually cataloged under *nm*(1) in the *User's Reference Manual*.

The ctime Function

The *ctime* function is used to the value of the time-stamp field in the COFF header file to an ASCII string representing the date and time.

The *ctime* function is used because the time-stamp value is the number of seconds since 00:00:00 Greenwich Mean Time, Jan. 1, 1970. To most people, this value is quite meaningless, and the conversion provided by the *ctime* function is very much appreciated.

To set the value of the time-stamp, use the *time* function. The time function returns a long value that is the number of seconds since time began for UNIX.

The *ctime* function is usually cataloged under *ctime*(3C) in the *User's Reference Manual*, while *time* is cataloged under *time*(2) in the same manual.

The COFF Library

libld.a is a library of special functions for working with COFF files: object, executable, and archive.

libld.a is intended to provide uniform access and handling of COFF files. The functions in *libld.a* are described in section (3X) of the *User's Reference Manual*.

The functions in *libld.a* implement reading of COFF file headers, sections, line numbers, relocation entries, string table and symbol table. The *libld.a* functions depend on the standard COFF file headers; therefore, any application that uses *libld.a* functions needs the standard COFF include files, and the *libld.a* header, *ldfcn.h*.

Applications of relatively meager complexity, such as the example code in this handbook, probably do not need the extensive support and organization provided by the libld functions. But integrated applications (such as development tools: from compilers to debuggers) typically use libld because of the organization and consistency of handling it provides.

The Basics of COFF

The Assembly Code
Relocation Process

COFF File Headers

Relocation Structures/
Relocation Process

The Linking Process

The COFF System in UNIX

Magic Numbers

The COFF Symbolic
Debug System

COFF and Shared Libraries

Utilities and Techniques for
Working with COFF Files

A Sample COFF Program

11

A Sample
COFF Program

Program Start: Header Files
Program Global Variables
The main() Body

This chapter presents a comprehensive source code example that demonstrates virtually all possible manipulations to the various COFF structures.

The source code example can serve as the foundation for many COFF-related programming tasks: from developing a utility for creating a file containing a program's raw data that are suitable for downloading to a PROM programmer, to a sophisticated COFF file editor program.

The example program presented in this chapter is a working program. The program illustrates how to access every region of the COFF file, and when executed, outputs the contents of the COFF file in an orderly fashion.

In many cases the coding is designed for tutorial clarity; not necessarily for optimal speed of execution. The areas where changes can be made in order to improve execution speed are noted in the descriptions of the code. Unless an application is used to process thousands of COFF files, the coding techniques used in the sample program are quite adequate.

If you wish to enter the program and try it, simply enter the source code fragments as presented.* Though every effort has been made to insure that the code is portable, no warranty is claimed in regards to the efficacy of this example program, or its universal reliability.

Program Start: Header Files

Any application program that works with COFF files needs to include the following header files:

```
#include <stdio.h>
#include <time.h>    /* Used for ctime function */

/* Headers for working with COFF files */

#include <aouthdr.h>
#include <filehdr.h>
#include <scnhdr.h>
#include <linenum.h>
#include <reloc.h>
#include <syms.h>
```

The first include file, *stdio.h,* is needed for general I/O purposes, such as opening and reading the COFF file. The second include file, *time.h,* is needed because the **ctime** function is used to convert the value in file header time-stamp field to an ASCII string representing the date/time.

---

*You can copy the example file to your system by anonymous FTP from *uunet.uu.net* (use binary transfer mode, *cd nutshell/coff* and get the file *example.c.Z*). Or, use anonymous UUCP (call UUNET at 1-900-468-7727, login as "uucp" with no password, and copy the file *uunet!˜ftp/nutshell/coff/example.c.Z*; as of this writing, the cost is 40 cents per minute). Once you have the file, use the command *uncompress example.c.Z* to create the *example.c* file.

The remaining include files contain COFF file structure declarations and mnemonic defines. The COFF definition has seven related include files, but only six have to be included (usually) in the program. This is because the header file *storclass.h* is included by the *syms.h* header file.

Program Global Variables

After the include files, the program needs the definition of its global variables. And even though the COFF structures are quite complex and varied, surprisingly few global variables are needed for most applications.

The following seven global variables completely satisfy the example program's needs:

```
        /* Global variables */

long num_sections; /* Number of section */
long section_seek; /* Used to seek to first section */

long symptr;       /* File pointer to symbol table entries */
long num_symbols;  /* Number of symbols */

char *str_tab;     /* Pointer to start of string char. array */
long str_length;   /* Length in bytes of string array */

FILE *fd;          /* COFF file descriptor */
```

A little reflection on the nature of the COFF file can easily justify these few global variables.

Most applications are interested in the information associated with the COFF file's sections. The number of sections is contained in the file header; therefore, it is saved as a global variable, num_sections, for use by the function that processes the sections. The global variable section_seek is also used by the section processing function. This is because the location of the first section header is a determined by information in the file header. This fact is clearly illustrated in the source code fragment that reads the headers.

The variables for the symbol table and the string table are global for the same reason as the section related global variables: their values are determined while reading the file headers. The fd FILE variable is global because several different functions read specific regions of the COFF file.

The main() Body

In general, access to the entire COFF file can be consolidated in the following few functions:

```
main(argc,argv)
int    argc;
char *argv[];
{
        fd = fopen(argv[1], "r");
        if (fd == 0) exit(0);

        read_headers();
        read_sections();
        read_strings();
        read_symbols();
        exit(0);
}
```

Each function processes a special region of the COFF file. These functions basically perform a read-COFF-file-structure/print-data loop for their specific areas. An application such as a COFF file editor consists of the same functions, except that the read sequences create an image of the COFF file in memory. These structures in memory can be modified as needed, and then written to an output file. Examples of how to create portions of the COFF file in memory are presented later on in this chapter.

The read_headers Function

The read_headers function reads the file header and the optional header. This function has the following code:

```
read_headers()
{
FILHDR   file_header; /* File header structure */
AOUTHDR    optional_header;/* Optional header structure */

    fread(&file_header, sizeof(FILHDR), 1, fd);

    printf("FILE HEADER VALUES\n");
    printf("f_magic  = 0%o\n", file_header.f_magic);
    printf("f_nscns  = %d\n",file_header.f_nscns);
    printf("f_timdat = %s",ctime(&file_header.f_timdat));
    printf("f_symptr = %d\n",file_header.f_symptr);
    printf("f_nsyms  = %d\n",file_header.f_nsyms);
    printf("f_opthdr = %d\n",file_header.f_opthdr);
    printf("f_flags  = 0%o\n",file_header.f_flags);

       /* Save the global values */

    num_sections = file_header.f_nscns;
    num_symbols  = file_header.f_nsyms;
    symptr       = file_header.f_symptr;

    if (file_header.f_opthdr)
    {
        fread(&optional_header,sizeof(AOUTHDR),1,fd);

        printf("OPTIONAL HEADER VALUES\n");
        printf("magic      = 0%o\n", optional_header.magic);
        printf("vstamp     = %d\n",optional_header.vstamp);
        printf("tsize      = %d\n",optional_header.tsize);
        printf("dsize      = %d\n",optional_header.dsize);
        printf("bsize      = %d\n",optional_header.bsize);
        printf("entry      = 0x%x\n",optional_header.entry);
        printf("text_start = 0x%x\n",optional_header.text_start);
        printf("data_start = 0x%x\n",optional_header.data_start);
        printf("flags      = 0x%x\n",optional_header.flags);
    }

    /* File offset for first section headers */
    section_seek = FILHSZ + file_header.f_opthdr;
}
```

The first thing to note is the use of header file declared symbols and defined values. All header-declared symbols and defined values are represented in upper-case. The header files are a great convenience since all of the needed structures are declared in the header files. The first two lines of this function are all that is required to define the needed structures to hold the file header and optional header contents.

The second thing to note is how the output of the optional header is handled. The function tests the size of the optional header to see if it is greater than zero. It is not uncommon for object files to completely lack an optional header. In most implementations, it is the linker that provides the optional header.

Lastly, note how the `section_seek` value is calculated. The first section header is located immediately after the optional header, if present, and the defined value `FILHSZ` is used instead of `sizeof(FILHDR)`. Always check the header files for explicit definitions of structure size. Use the explicitly defined value if present.

The read_sections Function

The `read_sections` function processes the section headers and other relevant section information. The code for `read_sections` is:

```
read_sections()
{
SCNHDR   sh;     /* Section header structure */
RELOC    re;     /* Relocation entry structure */
LINENO   le;     /* Line number entry structure */
char     *raw_data;
int      i,j;

       for (i = 0; i < num_sections; i++)
           {
           fseek(fd,section_seek,0);
           fread(&sh,sizeof(SCNHDR),1,fd);
           section_seek += sizeof(SCNHDR);

           printf("\n %s - SECTION HEADER - \n",sh.s_name);
           printf("s_paddr   = 0x%x\n",sh.s_paddr);
           printf("s_vaddr   = 0x%x\n",sh.s_vaddr);
           printf("s_size    = %d\n",sh.s_size);
           printf("s_scnptr  = %d\n",sh.s_scnptr);
           printf("s_relptr  = %d\n",sh.s_relptr);
           printf("s_lnnoptr = %d\n",sh.s_lnnoptr);
           printf("s_nreloc  = %d\n",sh.s_nreloc);
           printf("s_nlnno   = %d\n",sh.s_nlnno);
           printf("s_flags   = 0x%x\n",sh.s_flags);
```

```
/* Output raw data only for text and data sections */
if (strcmp(sh.s_name,".bss"))
        {
        raw_data = (char *)malloc(sh.s_size);
        fseek(fd,sh.s_scnptr,0);
        fread(raw_data,sh.s_size,1,fd);

        printf("RAW DATA\n");
        j=0;
        while(j<sh.s_size)
                {
                printf("%1x",(*raw_data>>4)&0xf);
                printf("%1x ",(*raw_data&0xf));
                *raw_data++; j++;
                if (j%16==0) printf("\n");
                    }
        printf("\n");
        free(raw_data-j);
        }

    if (sh.s_nreloc)
        {
        printf("\n RELOCATION ENTRIES\n");
        fseek(fd,sh.s_relptr,0);
        j=0;
        while(j<sh.s_nreloc)
                {
                fread(&re,RELSZ,1,fd);
                printf("r_vaddr = 0x%x",re.r_vaddr);
                    printf(" r_symndx = %d\n",re.r_symndx);
                j++;
                }
        }

    if (sh.s_nlnno)
            {
            printf("\n LINE NUMBER ENTRIES \n");
            fseek(fd,sh.s_lnnoptr,0);
            j=0;
            while(j<sh.s_nlnno)
                    {
                    fread(&le,LINESZ,1,fd);
                    if (le.l_lnno == 0)
printf("function address 0x%x\n",le.l_addr.l_symndx);
                    else
```

```
printf("line# %d at address 0x%x\n",\
       le.l_lnno, le.l_addr.l_paddr);
          j++;
          }
    }


}
}
```

The `read_sections` function has several worthwhile points to notice.

First, the `read_sections` function has several good examples of how file-offset pointers are used. This includes the use of the `s_scnptr, s_relptr`, and `s_lnnoptr` values.

Second, the `read_sections` function shows how to access the section's raw data, something that is usually of some importance to many COFF application programs. Note how memory is allocated for the raw data. The technique is generally applicable to any area of the COFF file. For instance, the following code can be used to create an array of relocation entries:

```
RELOC *re; /* pointer to relocation entry structure */

re = calloc(1, RELSZ*s_nreloc);
fread(re, RELSZ*s_nreloc, 1, fp);
while (s_nreloc)
      {
      /* process a relocation entry*/
      /* and increment pointer to next entry */
      re = (RELOC *)((int)re + RELSZ);
      }
```

Note that the amount of allocated memory is equal to the `RELSZ` times the number of relocation entries. The same is true for the size of the `fread`. Also note that when the `re` structure pointer is incremented, the explicit casting is needed since the `sizeof` function is not used.

An alternative to creating an array of a certain structure is to create a linked list of those structures. The following code briefly outlines the creation of a linked list of section header structures:

```
struct s_list
{
SCNHDR sh;
struct s_list *next;
} *first, *ptr;
        ptr = calloc(1,sizeof(struct s_list));
        first = ptr;
        for (i = 0; i < num_sections; i++)
            {
            fread(ptr->sh,sizeof(SCNHDR),1,fp);
            if (i==(num_sections - 1))
                ptr->next = 0;
            else
                {
                ptr->next = calloc(1,sizeof(struct s_list));
                ptr = ptr->next;
                }
            }
```

This is fairly standard list creation code. Note that the starting point is explicitly saved. Variations to this theme can be found in many C programming style books.

Whether an array is needed, or a linked list, depends on the type of operations that are to be performed on the data. Arrays are suitable for a scan/modify type of operation on a fixed number of entries. Linked list are much more suitable if additions or deletions of entries are to be performed.

Operations in memory-created portions of the COFF file are usually faster than the incremental read file technique used by the sample program. But the coding is complicated because dynamic memory allocation is needed. The simpler and slower, technique of the example code presents greater tutorial clarity.

The read_strings Function

The read_strings function processes the string table. The string table is processed before the symbol table because some symbol names might reside in the string table. The read_strings function creates a string table in memory that is easily available to the read_symbols function. The read_strings function has the following code:

```
read_strings()
{
int    strings;
char   *str_ptr;

       strings = symptr+sizeof(SYMENT)*num_symbols;
       fseek(fd,strings,0);
       fread(&str_length,4,1,fd);
       if (str_length) {
            printf("\n STRING TABLE DUMP\n");
            str_length-=4;
            str_tab = (char *)malloc(str_length);
            fseek(fd,(strings+4),0);
            fread(str_tab,str_length,1,fd);
            str_ptr=str_tab;
            do   {
                 printf("%s\n",str_ptr);
                 while(*str_ptr++ !='\0');
                 }
            while(str_ptr<(str_tab+str_length));
            }
}
```

The first thing to note is how the pointer to the string table is calculated. The string table pointer calculation includes the use of two of the global variables. Next, notice that the string table array, `str_tab`, does not include the first four bytes of the string table. Instead, these first four bytes are read and then stored in the global variable `str_length`. Also note that the loop to output the strings is relatively simple since the strings are all null terminated. This allows a simple application of the `printf` function. Access to the string table is global because of the `str_tab` global variable.

The read_symbols Function

The `read_symbols` function has the following code:

```
read_symbols()
{
SYMENT      se;
AUXENT      ae;
int    i;
int    j;

       fseek(fd,symptr,0);
```

```
printf("\n SYMBOL TABLE ENTRIES\n");
i = 0;
while (i   != num_symbols)
        {
        fread(&se,sizeof(SYMENT),1,fd);
        print_se(&se);  i++;
        for (j = 0; j < se.n_numaux; j++)
                {
                fread(&ae,sizeof(AUXENT),1,fd);
                print_ae(&ae);
                i++;
                }
        }
}
```

Note that this function uses the global variable num_symbols. This
function uses two other functions: one to process symbol table entries,
and one to process auxiliary entries. The auxiliary entries are processed
as a loop that is controlled by the symbol table entry's n_numaux
field. Though the size of the read is specified by the respective sizes of
SYMENT and AUXENT, in most cases these two are equal.

The Symbol Table Processing Function

The symbol table processing function analyzes the individual symbol
table entries. It has the following code:

```
print_se(se)
SYMENT  *se;
{
int i;
        if (se->n_zeroes)
                {
                for ( i = 0; i < 8; i++)
                        {
                        if ((se->n_name[i]>0x1f)&&(se->n_name[i]<0x7f))
                                printf("%c",se->n_name[i]);
                        else
                                printf(" ");
                        }
                }
        else
                printf("%s",&str_tab[(se->_n._n_n._n_offset-4)]);

        printf(" n_scnum=%d ",se->n_scnum);

        switch (se->n_type & 0xf)
                {
```

```
            case T_CHAR:    printf("T_CHAR"); break;
            case T_SHORT:   printf("T_SHORT"); break;
            case T_INT:     printf("T_INT"); break;
            case T_LONG:    printf("T_LONG"); break;
            case T_FLOAT:   printf("T_FLOAT"); break;
            case T_DOUBLE:  printf("T_DOUBLE"); break;
            case T_STRUCT:  printf("T_STRUCT"); break;
            case T_UNION:   printf("T_UNION"); break;
            case T_ENUM:    printf("T_ENUM"); break;
            case T_MOE:     printf("T_MOE"); break;
            case T_UCHAR:   printf("T_UCHAR"); break;
            case T_USHORT:  printf("T_USHORT"); break;
            case T_UINT:    printf("T_UINT"); break;
            case T_ULONG:   printf("T_ULONG"); break;
            default:        printf("n_type=%d",se->n_type&0xf); break;
            }

    if (ISFCN(se->n_type))
            printf(",DT_FCN ");
    else
            if (ISPTR(se->n_type))
                    printf(",DT_PTR ");
    else
            if (ISARY(se->n_type))
                    printf(",DT_ARY ");

    switch (se->n_sclass)
        {
        case C_NULL   : printf(" C_NULL=0x%x",se->n_value); break;
        case C_STAT   : printf(" C_STAT=0x%x",se->n_value); break;
        case C_EXT    : printf(" C_EXT=0x%x",se->n_value); break;
        case C_AUTO   : printf(" C_AUTO=0x%x",se->n_value); break;
        case C_FILE   : printf(" C_FILE"); break;
        case C_STRTAG : printf(" C_STRTAG"); break;
        case C_EOS    : printf(" C_EOS=0x%x",se->n_value); break;
        case C_FCN    : printf(" C_FCN=0x%x",se->n_value); break;
        case C_EFCN   : printf(" C_EFCN=0x%x",se->n_value); break;
        default       : printf(" n_sclass=0x%x",se->n_sclass); break;
        }

    printf(" n_numaux=%d\n",se->n_numaux);
}
```

The first point of interest is the code that outputs the symbol's name. There are two interesting aspects. First, notice how the decision is made as to whether the _n_name field is an offset or an ASCII string. Second, note that when the _n_name field is printed as an ASCII string, the output is one character at a time, up to the maximum eight. This is because the _n_name field is null terminated only for names less than eight characters long. Unambiguous output is possible only when output is one character at a time.

The rest of the symbol table entry code is fairly unremarkable with the exception that it provides several examples of how to use the numerous defined values from the several symbolic information include files. As can be seen, the switch statement plays a prominent role in implementing efficient and manageable code to deal with the many variations of symbol type and storage class.

The Auxiliary Entry Processing Function

The auxiliary entry processing function reads the individual auxiliary entries. It has the following code:

```
print_ae(ae)
char *ae;
{
int i;
        printf(" Aux. = ");
        for( i = 1; i <= AUXESZ; i++ )
            {
            printf("%1x", (*ae>>4)&0xf);
            printf("%1x ", (*ae&0xf));
            *ae++;
            }

        printf("\n");
}
```

This function does not attempt to discriminate between the various types of auxiliary entries: it simply outputs the auxiliary entry as a stream of hexadecimal byte values.

A

COFF Structure Quick Reference and Summary

Introduction

This appendix contains a quick reference and summary of the most important and often encountered COFF structures and their related mnemonics.

The structures are introduced by their declared names, and the summary lists the structures fields along with a brief description of the field. Relevant mnemonics are also listed, and for the sake of convenience, some figures are reproduced here.

Note that the information presented here does not include implementation-dependent deviations; check your system specific COFF documentation, or COFF related header files for possible deviations and enhancements.

Structure filehdr

The file header structure, **filehdr**, is declared in the file *filehdr.h* and has the following fields:

Table A-1: File Header Structure Fields

Field Name	Type	Description
f_magic	unsigned short	Environment identifying magic number.
f_nscns	unsigned short	Number of sections.
f_timdat	long	UNIX format time stamp.
f_symptr	long	File pointer to start of symbol table.
f_nsyms	long	Number of symbol table entries.
f_opthdr	unsigned short	Size of optional header in bytes.
f_flags	unsigned short	File status flags.

The *filehdr.h* file contains the following useful defines:

```
#define    FILHDR    struct filehdr
#define    FILHSZ    sizeof(FILHDR)
```

Table A-2: f_flags Values

Mnemonic	Flag Field Bit	Meaning
F_RELFLG	0000001	The COFF file does not contain relocation information.
F_EXEC	0000002	The COFF file is executable.
F_LNNO	0000004	Line numbers have been stripped from the COFF file.
L_SYMS	0000010	Local symbols have been stripped from the COFF file.

Note: the **f_flags** field usually contains some implementation-dependent information. This information typically is reserved for specifying architectural information, or special hardware dependent information.

Figure A-1 diagrams the uses of the **filehdr** structure.

Structure aouthdr

The *aouthdr.h* file declares the following fields for the optional header:

Table A-3: Optional Header Structure Fields

Field Name	Type	Description
magic	short	Runtime status magic number.
vstamp	short	Optional version stamp.
tsize	long	Size of machine code in bytes.
dsize	long	Size of initialized data in bytes.
bsize	long	Size of uninitialized data in bytes.
entry	long	Starting address of program execution.
text_start	long	Runtime starting address of machine code.
data_start	long	Runtime starting address of program data.

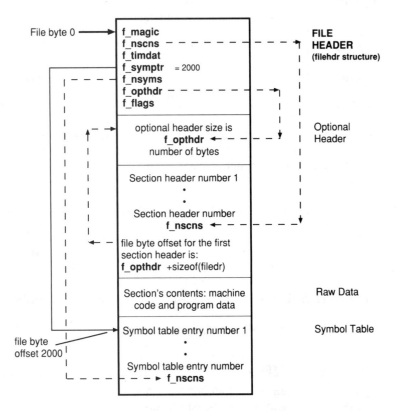

File byte 0 ⟶

f_magic
f_nscns — — — — — — — ⟶ **FILE**
f_timdat   **HEADER**
f_symptr = 2000   (filehdr structure)
f_nsyms
f_opthdr — — — — — — ⟶
f_flags

optional header size is   Optional
f_opthdr ⟵ — — — ⟶   Header
number of bytes

Section header number 1
•
•
Section header number
f_nscns ⟵ — — — — ⟶

file byte offset for the first
section header is:
f_opthdr +sizeof(filedr)

Section's contents: machine   Raw Data
code and program data

Symbol table entry number 1   Symbol Table
•
•
file byte
offset 2000
Symbol table entry number
— — ⟶ **f_nscns**

Figure A-1. File header components and structural relationships

The **aouthdr** structure is typedef'd as AOUTHDR.

Implementation-dependent **aouthdr** field values are usually documented in the file *a.out.h* in the */usr/include* directory.

Figure A-2 shows how the **aouthdr** fields are used.

Structure scnhdr

The **scnhdr** structure is declared in the file *scnhdr.h*. The **scnhdr** structure has the following fields:

Table A-4: scnhdr Structure Fields

Field Name	Type	Description
s_name[8]	char	Section's name.
s_paddr	long	Physical address.
s_vaddr	long	Virtual address
s_size	long	Section's size in bytes.
s_scnptr	long	File pointer to section's raw data.
s_relptr	long	File pointer to section's relocation entries.
s_lnnoptr	long	File pointer to section's line numbers.
s_nreloc	unsigned short	Number of relocation entries.
s_nlnno	unsigned short	Number of line number entries.
s_flags	long	Section type and content flag.

The *scnhdr.h* file contains the following useful defines:

```
#define SCNHDR struct scnhdr
#define SCNHSZ sizeof(SCNHDR)
```

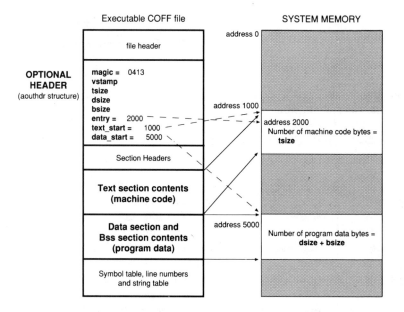

Executable COFF file   SYSTEM MEMORY

This diagram shows how the various fields in the optional header are used in mapping the executable file's image into system memory. Typically, the optional header fields are meaningful only for executable files.

Figure A-2. The executable COFF file in memory

Table A-5: s_flags Values

Mnemonic	Meaning
STYP_REG	Regular section, either text, data, bss, info, or lib type.
STYP_TEXT	Text section: allocated, relocated, and loaded.
STYP_DATA	Data section: allocated, relocated, and loaded.
STYP_BSS	Bss sections are only allocated.
STYP_INFO	Comment section: not allocated, not relocated, and not loaded.
STYP_LIB	Section contains shared-library relocation information.
STYP_DSECT	A dummy section type created by the assembler's
STYP_PAD	Alignment spacing between regular sections.

Figure A-3 diagrams the **scnhdr** structure's role within the COFF framework.

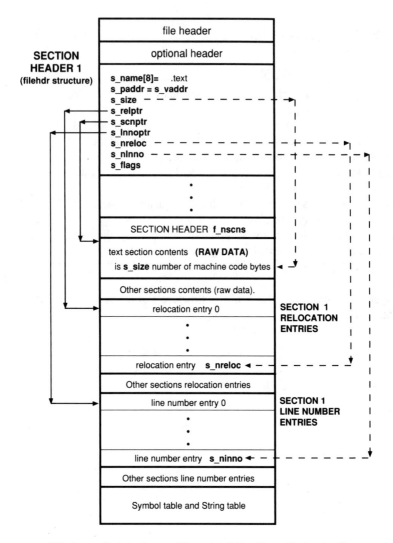

This diagram illustrates the use of the various fields of the section header. The section shown in this example is a text section. The usage of the fields is analogous for the data section. However, since the bss section does not have raw data, relocation entries, and line numbers, has those relevant fields set to zero.

Figure A-3. Section header schema

Structure reloc

The file *reloc.h* contains the **reloc** structure's declaration. The major fields are listed in Table A-6:

Table A-6: reloc Structure Fields

Field Name	Type	Description
r_vaddr	long	Pointer to an area in raw data that represents a referenced address.
r_symndx	long	Index into symbol table.
r_type	unsigned short	Type of address reference.

The **r_type** field is extremely implementation-dependent. Check your *reloc.h* file for specific address types.

Figure A-4 diagrams the **reloc** structure's components in action.

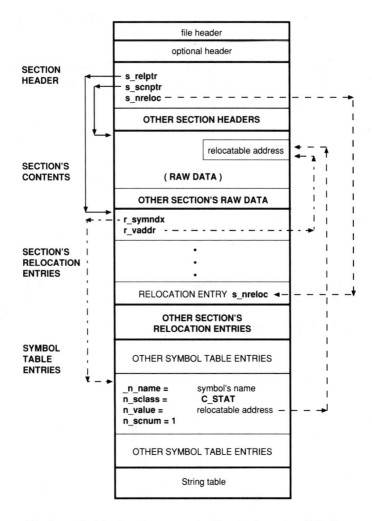

This diagram illustrates the major components of the relocation system. Notice the different uses for the pointer field values. For example, r_vaddr is a byte offset relative to the start of the section's contents, and points to the area in raw data that is relocated (patched). r_symndx is an index value into the symbol table. On the other hand, s_scnptr is a file pointer to the start of the section's raw data.

Figure A-4. Relocation system components

Structure syment

The symbol table structure, `syment`, is declared in the file *syms.h*. The major fields of this structure are listed in Table A-7:

Table A-7: Symbol Table Structure Fields

Field Name	Type	Description
_n_name[SYMNMLEN]	char	Symbol name, or pointer into string table if symbol name is greater than SYMNMLEN.
n_value	long	Symbol's value: dependent on section number, storage class, and type.
n_scnum	short	Section number.
n_type	unsigned short	Symbolic type.
n_sclass	char	Storage class.
n_numaux	char	Number of auxiliary entries.

Table A-8: n_scnum Values

Mnemonic	Value	Meaning
N_DEBUG	–2	n_value represents special symbolic debug information as created by an assembler symbolic directive.
N_ABS	–1	n_value is an absolute value.
N_UNDEF	0	n_value is meaningless since the symbol is an undefined external symbol.
N_SCNUM	>0	n_value is a positive integer representing the section number where the symbol is defined.

Table A-9: n_type (Fundamental) Values

Mnemonic	Value	Meaning
T_NULL	0	no type
T_VOID	1	void
T_CHAR	2	character
T_SHORT	2	short integer
T_INT	4	integer
T_LONG	5	long integer
T_FLOAT	6	floating point
T_DOUBLE	7	double word
T_STRUCT	8	structure
T_UNION	9	union
T_ENUM	10	enumeration
T_MOE	11	member of enumeration
T_UCHAR	12	unsigned character
T_USHORT	13	unsigned short
T_UINT	14	unsigned integer
T_ULONG	15	unsigned long

Table A-10: n_type (Derived) Values

Mnemonic	Value	Meaning
DT_NON	0	no derived type
DT_PTR	1	pointer
DT_FCN	2	function
DT_ARY	3	array

Table A-11: n_sclass Values

Storage Class	Section Numbers	Value Interpretation
C_EXT	N_ABS, N_UNDEF, N_SCNUM	External symbol relocatable address.
C_AUTO	N_ABS	Automatic (stack) variable. Specifies stack (frame) offset.
C_REG	N_ABS	Register variable. Specifies a register number.
C_LABEL	N_UNDEF, N_SCNUM	Go to label's relocatable address.
C_MOS	N_ABS	Specifies nth member of structure.
C_ARG	N_ABS	Specifies nth function argument.
C_STRTAG	N_DEBUG	Structure tagname entry.
C_MOU	N_ABS	Specifies nth member of union.
C_UNTAG	N_DEBUG	Union tagname entry.
C_TPDEF	N_DEBUG	Type definition entry.
C_ENTAG	N_DEBUG	Enumeration tagname entry.
C_MOE	N_ABS	Specifies nth member of enumeration.
C_REGPARM	N_ABS	Register parameter. Specifies register number.
C_FIELD	N_ABS	Specifies nth bit in a bit field.
C_BLOCK	N_SCNUM	Relocatable address for either the beginning of a block (.bb), or end of a block (.eb).
C_FCN	N_SCNUM	Relocatable address for either the beginning of a function (.bf), or end of a function (.ef).
C_EOS	N_ABS	End of structure entry.
C_FILE	N_DEBUG	Symbol table index.

n_name Values

The following defines in file *syms.h* are useful for handling the dual interpretation of the _n_name symbol name field:

```
#define n_name      _n._n_name
#define n_nptr      _n._n_nptr[1]
#define n_zeroes    _n._n_n._n_zeroes
#define n_offset    _n._n_n._n_offset
```

Figure A-5 diagrams the n_name field use in the case where the interpretation is for a long symbolic name in the string table.

Structure lineno

The **lineno** structure is declared in file *linenum.h* and has the following fields:

Table A-12: lineno Structure Fields

Field Name	Type	Description
l_symndx	long	Index into symbol table if l_lnno == 0.
l_paddr	long	Break-pointable address if l_lnno > 0.
l_lnno	unsigned short	Line number.

The *linenum.h* file has the following defines:

```
#define LINENO  struct lineno
#define LINESZ  6  /* sizeof(LINENO) */
```

Figure A-6 diagrams the dual interpretation of the first field in the **lineno** structure.

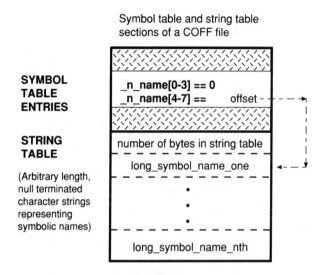

Symbol table and string table
sections of a COFF file

**SYMBOL
TABLE
ENTRIES**

_n_name[0-3] == 0
_n_name[4-7] ==   offset

**STRING
TABLE**

number of bytes in string table

long_symbol_name_one

(Arbitrary length,
null terminated
character strings
representing
symbolic names)

•
•
•

long_symbol_name_nth

If the first four characters of a symbol's name are null, the last four
characters represent an offset (relative to the start of the string table)
into the string table where the symbol's name is stored. Since the string
table entries are unstructured, symbols of any length can be stored.
Symbol names are terminated by a null character.

The first four bytes in the string table represent a long value that specifies
the number of bytes in the string table. An empty string table has a
length field, but the value stored there is 0.

Figure A-5. Long symbol-name storage

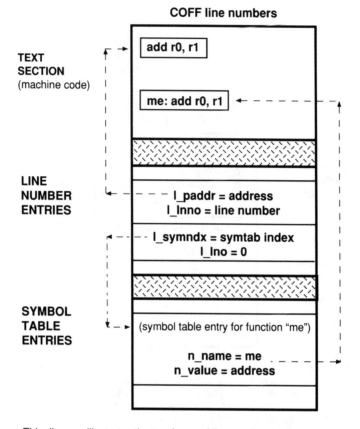

COFF line numbers

This diagram illustrates the two forms of line number entries. In both cases, the line number entry provides an address that can be used as a break point.

If l_lnno is greater than zero, the first field in the line number entry is interpreted as an address representing the first instruction for a line of source code.

If l_lnno is zero, the first field is interpreted as an index into the symbol table; in which case the n_value field of the symbol table entry is used as a break point address. This allows symbolic specification for break points.

Figure A-6. Line number entries

Symbol Table Figures

Figures A-7 through A-9 diagram the most important and complex components of the COFF symbolic system.

The figures summarize the symbol-table entry order, tagname entry schema, and the linked listed used for efficient implementation of debug information for functions and structures.

Structure ar_hdr

There is only one structure associated with archive files, and it is declared in the file *ar.h*. The archive structure has the following components:

Table A-13: Archive Structure Components

Field Name	Type	Description
ar_name[16]	char	Member's name.
ar_date[12]	char	Date archived.
ar_uid[6]	char	Creator's user ID.
ar_gid[6]	char	Creator's group ID.
ar_mode[8]	char	Access mode.
ar_size[10]	char	Member's size in bytes.
ar_fmag[2]	char	Magic string to end header.

Figure A-10 diagrams the use of the **ar_hdr** structure.

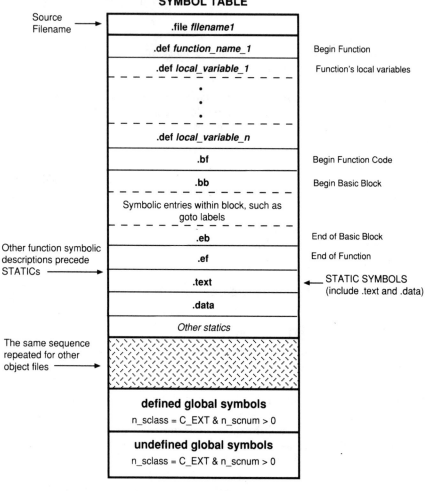

COFF
SYMBOL TABLE

Source Filename →

.file *fllename1*	
.def *function_name_1*	Begin Function
.def *local_variable_1*	Function's local variables
• • •	
.def *local_variable_n*	
.bf	Begin Function Code
.bb	Begin Basic Block
Symbolic entries within block, such as goto labels	
.eb	End of Basic Block
.ef	End of Function
.text	← STATIC SYMBOLS (include .text and .data)
.data	
Other statics	
defined global symbols n_sclass = C_EXT & n_scnum > 0	
undefined global symbols n_sclass = C_EXT & n_scnum > 0	

Other function symbolic descriptions precede STATICs →

The same sequence repeated for other object files →

This diagram illustrates the order of entries in the symbol table. Note that the order is based on two levels. The first, represented by the .file entry, is at the source file level. The second, represented by such entries as .bf and .bb, is at the structural level of the particular source file. The final entries, the globals, are common to all source files. (Auxiliary entries are not shown.) Also, .bb - .eb are used only for basic blocks and are not present if a function does not have basic blocks.)

Figure A-7. Symbol Table Order

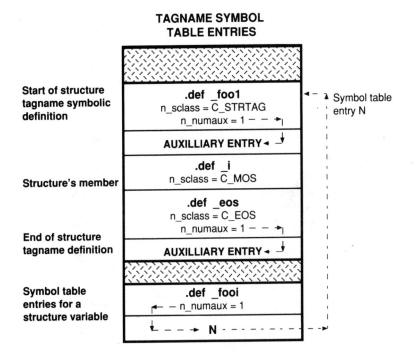

**TAGNAME SYMBOL
TABLE ENTRIES**

This diagram illustrates a structure type variable's relationship with its tagname symbol table entries. The symbol table auxiliary entry for a structure variable has an index value that points to the structure's tagname definition. The structure's tagname definition consists of a series of symbol table entries that completely characterize the structure.

Figure A-8. Tagname entry schema

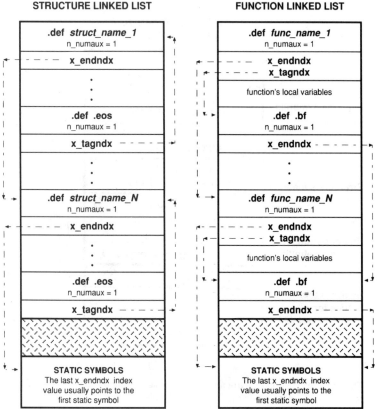

STRUCTURE LINKED LIST   FUNCTION LINKED LIST

This diagram illustrates how auxiliary entries are used to implement linked lists of symbolic information. The left-hand diagram shows a structure linked list. The right-hand diagram shows a function linked list.

Figure A-9. Auxiliary entry linked list structure

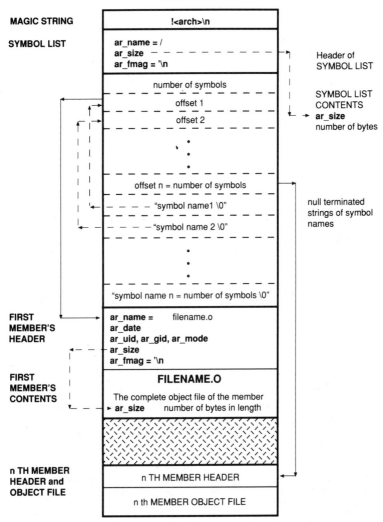

ARCHIVE FILE

MAGIC STRING — !<arch>\n

SYMBOL LIST

ar_name = /
ar_size
ar_fmag = '\n

> Header of
> SYMBOL LIST

number of symbols

offset 1

offset 2

> SYMBOL LIST
> CONTENTS
> **ar_size**
> number of bytes

• • •

offset n = number of symbols

"symbol name1 \0"

"symbol name 2 \0"

> null terminated
> strings of symbol
> names

• • •

"symbol name n = number of symbols \0"

FIRST MEMBER'S HEADER

ar_name =   filename.o
ar_date
ar_uid, ar_gid, ar_mode
ar_size
ar_fmag = '\n

FIRST MEMBER'S CONTENTS

FILENAME.O

The complete object file of the member
ar_size   number of bytes in length

n TH MEMBER HEADER and OBJECT FILE

n TH MEMBER HEADER

n th MEMBER OBJECT FILE

The point to note is that the symbol list offsets point to the header of the archive file member where the symbol is defined. This allows efficient searching of library files.

Figure A-10. The archive file structure

Index

debug request (–*g*)
declarations, symbolic 6
declared symbols 16 - 17
.def assembler directive 87, 104, 116
default
  link process 28
  optional header values 28
defined symbols 16 - 17
derived types 118 - 119
dot files 8
.dsect assembler directive 69
dump utility 132

E

.eb assembler directive 104
.ef assembler directive 87, 104, 116
.endef assembler directive 87
environment field 122
.eos assembler directive 109, 113
executable file
  definition 5
  normal 27, 28
extensibility
  C vs. Pascal 122 - 123
  with COFF 11
external symbol
  explicit 17
  implicit 17

F

fake tagname 112
f_flags field 24 - 26, 82
field values
  absolute value xv
  file-offset xv
  relative-offset xv

.file
  assembler directive 104
  symbol table entry 106, 108
file header 21, 22 - 26, 30, 33, 34
  fields 23 - 24
  structure 22 - 24
  summary 33 - 34
file pointer value 30 - 33
file section
  bss 9
  data 9
  text 9
file space, saving 18
file-offset xv
  representation xvi
files
  archive 2, 8, 63, 66, 73 - 78, 81, 133
  dot 8
  header include 22
  normal executable 27, 28
  object 2, 5, 7, 8, 16, 18, 25, 26, 34, 35, 55, 56, 59, 63, 70, 73, 78, 126, 133, 141
  relocatable 35
  source 3, 6, 8, 17, 28, 43, 50, 58, 71, 84, 85, 101, 103, 104, 121, 123
F_LNNO field 25
f_magic number 23, 27, 34, 81 - 82
f_nscns field 23
f_nsymptr field 34
f_nsyms field xv, 24, 34, 56
f_opthdr field 24, 33
F_RELFLG field 25
fseek function 39
f_symptr field xv, 24, 30, 56
f_timdat field 23
functions
  ctime 24
  fseek 39
  time 24

non-decomposable data 118
normal executable files 27, 28
n_sclass field 46, 47, 84, 85, 86, 87, 88, 96, 103
n_scnum field 46, 49, 58 - 62, 72, 85, 86, 98, 100, 103
N_SCNUM flag 99, 100, 105, 110
n_type field 84, 85, 86, 87, 88
N_UNDEF flag 99, 100, 105, 110
n_value field 46, 47, 49, 50, 52, 58 - 62, 72, 85, 86, 87, 88, 92, 94, 96- 103
_n_zeroes field 89

O

object files 2, 8, 16, 25, 35, 63, 73, 78, 126, 141
  and archiver 7
  and linker parameters 7
  assembler-created 26, 34
  definition 5
  input 55, 56, 59, 70
  multiple 55, 56
  partial linking 25
  relocatable 2
  space saving 18, 133
od utility 132
optional header 21, 24, 26 - 30, 28, 29, 33, 34
  default values 28
  fields 27 - 29
  structure 26 - 29
output map 39

P

patching 46
patching machine code (see updating)

portability of COFF 11
privacy 50

R

−*r* retain option
raw data 23, 39
read_headers 88, 96, 139 - 141
read_sections 141 - 144
read_strings 144 - 145
read_symbols 145 - 146
regular section 68
relative-offset xv
  representation xvi
relocatable
  address 49, 61
  code after linking 52
  code before linking 50 - 51
  code dynamics 42 - 44
  files 35
  object files 2
relocated sections
  data 69
  dummy 70
  shared library information 69
  text 68
relocation 2, 6, 35 - 53
  address calculation 50 - 53
  definition 12
  entries 40 - 42
  entry values 42 - 44
  information 6, 15 - 17
  information area 39
  of data sections 64 - 65
  of sections 68
resolution 6
retain option (−*r*)

Books That Help People Get More Out of Computers

If you want more information about our books, or want to know where to buy them, we're happy to send it.

☐ Send me a free catalog of titles.

☐ What bookstores in my area carry your books (U.S. and Canada only)?

☐ Where can I buy your books outside the U.S. and Canada?

☐ Send me information about consulting services for documentation or programming.

Name _____

Address _____

_____

City _____

State, ZIP _____

Country _____

NAME _____

COMPANY _____

ADDRESS _____

CITY _____ STATE _____ ZIP _____

BUSINESS REPLY MAIL

FIRST CLASS MAIL   PERMIT NO. 80   SEBASTOPOL, CA

POSTAGE WILL BE PAID BY ADDRESSEE

O'Reilly & Associates, Inc.

103 Morris Street Suite A
Sebastopol CA 95472-9902

About the Author

Gintaras Richard Gircys is founder and president of InfoServe Connections, a firm specializing in Internet connectivity for DOS users. Rich dates back to UNIX SVR3.0 and DOS 2.0 and is equally interested in both environments. In addition to the O'Reilly book, he has authored an extensive number of proprietary publications on various UNIX and DOS related topics.

When not playing with computers, Rich enjoys sailing the Monterey Bay, relaxing in his Santa Cruz mountain home, and exercising his four lazy cats. Rich graduated with honors in 1986 from San Jose State University; his degrees is a B.S. in Economics. If you can understand Economics, you can understand anything.

Colophon

Our look is the result of reader comments, our own experimentation, and feedback from distribution channels.

Distinctive covers complement our distinctive approach to technical topics, breathing personality and life into potentially dry subjects. UNIX and its attendant programs can be unruly beasts. Nutshell Handbooks help you tame them.

The animal featured on the cover of *Understanding and Using COFF* is a walrus. An Arctic marine mammal the size of a small car, the walrus is distinguished from the seal by its tusks; upper canines which grow to lengths of 15 inches or more. Walrus tusks have been frequently used as an alternative to elephant ivory in carvings. The walrus lives primarily in the water and on ice floes, only rarely coming ashore. In the water, it can dive to depths of 300 feet where it uses its tusks to scrape mollusks and other marine animals from the ocean floor. Lone males sometimes supplement this diet by killing and eating seals, and have been known, on occasion, to attack small boats and actively pursue and try to kill people in the water. In general, however, they are non-confrontational, attacking only if attacked, guarding young, or rutting.

Edie Freedman designed this cover and the entire UNIX bestiary that appears on other Nutshell Handbooks. The beasts themselves are adapted from 19th-century engravings from the Dover Pictorial Archive.

The text of this book is set in Times Roman; headings are Helvetica; examples are Courier. Text was prepared using SoftQuad's sqtroff text formatter. Figures are produced with a Macintosh. Printing is done on an Apple LaserWriter.

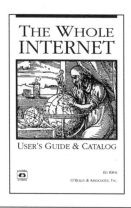

System Performance Tuning

By Mike Loukides

System Performance Tuning answers one of the most fundamental questions you can ask about your computer: "How can I get it to do more work without buying more hardware?" Anyone who has ever used a computer has wished that the system was faster, particularly at times when it was under heavy load.

If your system gets sluggish when you start a big job, if it feels as if you spend hours waiting for remote file access to complete, if your system stops dead when several users are active at the same time, you need to read this book. Some performance problems do require you to buy a bigger or faster computer, but many can be solved simply by making better use of the resources you already have.

336 pages, ISBN 0-937175-60-9

Essential System Administration

By Æleen Frisch

Like any other multi-user system, UNIX requires some care and feeding. *Essential System Administration* tells you how. This book strips away the myth and confusion surrounding this important topic and provides a compact, manageable introduction to the tasks faced by anyone responsible for a UNIX system.

If you use a stand-alone UNIX system, whether it's a PC or a workstation, you know how much you need this book: on these systems the fine line between a user and an administrator has vanished. Either you're both or you're in trouble. If you routinely provide administrative support for a larger shared system or a network of workstations, you will find this book indispensable. Even if you aren't directly responsible for system administration, you will find that understanding basic administrative functions greatly increases your ability to use UNIX effectively.

466 pages, ISBN 0-937175-80-3

Practical UNIX Security

By Simson Garfinkel & Gene Spafford

If you are a UNIX system administrator or user who needs to deal with security, you need this book.

Practical UNIX Security describes the issues, approaches, and methods for implementing security measures—spelling out what the varying approaches cost and require in the way of equipment. After presenting UNIX security basics and network security, this guide goes on to suggest how to keep intruders out, how to tell if they've gotten in, how to clean up after them, and even how to prosecute them. Filled with practical scripts, tricks and warnings, *Practical UNIX Security* tells you what you need to know to make your UNIX system as secure as it can be.

512 pages, ISBN 0-937175-72-2

Computer Security Basics

By Deborah Russell & G.T. Gangemi Sr.

There's a lot more consciousness of security today, but not a lot of understanding of what it means and how far it should go. This handbook describes complicated concepts like trusted systems, encryption and mandatory access control in simple terms.

For example, most U.S. government equipment acquisitions now require "Orange Book" (Trusted Computer System Evaluation Criteria) certification. A lot of people have a vague feeling that they ought to know about the Orange Book, but few make the effort to track it down and read it. *Computer Security Basics* contains a more readable introduction to the Orange Book—why it exists, what it contains, and what the different security levels are all about—than any other book or government publication.

464 pages
ISBN 0-937175-71-4

COMPUTER SECURITY BASICS

Deborah Russell and G. T. Gangemi Sr.
O'Reilly & Associates, Inc.

Managing UUCP and Usenet

10th Edition
By Tim O'Reilly & Grace Todino

For all its widespread use, UUCP is one of the most difficult UNIX utilities to master. Poor documentation, cryptic messages, and differences between various implementations make setting up UUCP links a nightmare for many a system administrator.

This handbook is meant for system administrators who want to install and manage the UUCP and Usenet software. It covers HoneyDanBer UUCP as well as standard Version 2 UUCP, with special notes on Xenix. As one reader noted over the Net, "Don't even TRY to install UUCP without it!"

368 pages, ISBN 0-937175-93-5

Using UUCP and Usenet

By Grace Todino & Dale Dougherty

Using UUCP shows how to communicate with both UNIX and non-UNIX systems using UUCP and *cu* or *tip*. It also shows how to read news and post your own articles and mail to other Usenet members. This handbook assumes that UUCP and Usenet links to other computer systems have already been established by your system administrator.

While clear enough for a novice, this book is packed with information that even experienced users will find indispensable. Take the mystery out of questions such as why files sent via UUCP don't always end up where you want them, how to find out the status of your file transfer requests, and how to execute programs remotely with *uux*.

210 pages, ISBN 0-937175-10-2

Understanding DCE

By Ward Rosenberry, David Kenney,
and Gerry Fisher

Understanding DCE is a technical and conceptual overview of OSF's Distributed Computing Environment for programmers and technical managers, marketing and sales people. Unlike many O'Reilly & Associates books, *Understanding DCE* has no hands-on programming elements. Instead, the book focuses on how DCE can be used to accomplish typical programming tasks and provides explanations to help the reader understand all the parts of DCE.

266 pages, ISBN 1-56592-005-8

Guide to Writing DCE Applications

By John Shirley

A hands-on programming guide to OSF's Distributed Computing Environment (DCE) for first-time DCE application programmers. This book is designed to help new DCE users make the transition from conventional, nondistributed applications programming to distributed DCE programming. Covers the IDL and ACF files, essential RPC calls, binding methods and the name service, server initialization, memory management, and selected advanced topics. Includes practical programming examples.

282 pages, ISBN 1-56592-004-X

Learning GNU Emacs

By Deb Cameron & Bill Rosenblatt

GNU Emacs is the most popular and widespread of the Emacs family of editors. It is also the most powerful and flexible. (Unlike all other text editors, GNU Emacs is a complete working environment—you can stay within Emacs all day without leaving.) This book tells you how to get started with the GNU Emacs editor. It will also "grow" with you: as you become more proficient, this book will help you learn how to use Emacs more effectively. It will take you from basic Emacs usage (simple text editing) to moderately complicated customization and programming.

The book is aimed at new Emacs users, whether or not they are programmers. Also useful for readers switching from other Emacs implementations to GNU Emacs.

442 pages, ISBN 0-937175-84-6

Learning the vi Editor

5th Edition
By Linda Lamb

For many users, working in the UNIX environment means using *vi*, a full-screen text editor available on most UNIX systems. Even those who know *vi* often make use of only a small number of its features. This is the complete guide to text editing with *vi*. Early chapters cover the basics; later chapters explain more advanced editing tools, such as *ex* commands and global search and replacement.

192 pages, ISBN 0-937175-67-6

Learning the UNIX Operating System

2nd Edition
By Grace Todino & John Strang

If you are new to UNIX, this concise introduction will tell you just what you need to get started, and no more. Why wade through a 600-page book when you can begin working productively in a matter of minutes?

Topics covered include:

- Logging in and logging out
- Managing UNIX files and directories
- Sending and receiving mail
- Redirecting input/output
- Pipes and filters
- Background processing
- Customizing your account

"If you have someone on your site who has never worked on a UNIX system and who needs a quick how-to, Nutshell has the right booklet. *Learning the UNIX Operating System* can get a newcomer rolling in a single session."—;login

84 pages, ISBN 0-937175-16-1

MH & xmh: E-mail for Users and Programmers

2nd Edition
By Jerry Peek

Customizing your e-mail environment can save you time and make communicating more enjoyable. *MH & xmh: E-mail for Users and Programmers* explains how to use, customize, and program with the MH electronic mail commands, available on virtually any UNIX system. The handbook also covers *xmh*, an X Window System client that runs MH programs.

The basics are easy. But MH lets you do much more than what most people expect an e-mail system to be able to do. This handbook is packed with explanations and useful examples of MH features, some of which the standard MH documentation only hints at.

728 pages, ISBN 1-56592-027-9

Guide to OSF/1: A Technical Synopsis

By O'Reilly & Associates Staff

OSF/1, Mach, POSIX, SVID, SVR4, X/Open, 4.4BSD, XPG, B-1 security, parallelization, threads, virtual file systems, shared libraries, streams, extensible loader, internationalization.... Need help sorting it all out? If so, then this technically competent introduction to the mysteries of the OSF/1 operating system is a book for you. In addition to its exposition of OSF/1, it offers a list of differences between OSF/1 and System V, Release 4 and a look ahead at what is coming in DCE.

This is not the usual O'Reilly how-to book. It will not lead you through detailed programming examples under OSF/1. Instead, it asks the prior question, What is the nature of the beast? It helps you figure out how to approach the programming task by giving you a comprehensive technical overview of the operating system's features and services, and by showing how they work together.

304 pages, ISBN 0-937175-78-1

POSIX Programmer's Guide

By Donald Lewine

Most UNIX systems today are POSIX-compliant because the Federal government requires it. Even OSF and UI agree on support for POSIX. However, given the manufacturer's documentation, it can be difficult to distinguish system-specific features from those features defined by POSIX.

The *POSIX Programmer's Guide*, intended as an explanation of the POSIX standard and as a reference for the POSIX.1 programming library, will help you write more portable programs. This guide is especially helpful if you are writing programs that must run on multiple UNIX platforms. This guide will also help you convert existing UNIX programs for POSIX-compliance.

640 pages, ISBN 0-937175-73-0

Managing NFS and NIS

By Hal Stern

A modern computer system that is not part of a network is an anomaly. But managing a network and getting it to perform well can be a problem. This book describes two tools that are absolutely essential to distributed computing environments: the Network Filesystem (NFS) and the Network Information System (formerly called the "yellow pages" or YP).

As popular as NFS is, it is a black box for most users and administrators. This book provides a comprehensive discussion of how to plan, set up, and debug an NFS network. It is the only book we're aware of that discusses NFS and network performance tuning. This book also covers the NFS automounter, network security issues, diskless workstations, and PC/NFS. It also tells you how to use NIS to manage your own database applications, ranging from a simple telephone list to controlling access to network services. If you are managing a network of UNIX systems, or are thinking of setting up a UNIX network, you can't afford to overlook this book.

436 pages, ISBN 0-937175-75-7

Power Programming with RPC

By John Bloomer

A distributed application is designed to access resources across a network. In a broad sense, these resources could be user input, a central database, configuration files, etc., that are distributed on various computers across the network rather than found on a single computer. RPC, or remote procedure calling, is the ability to distribute the execution of functions on remote computers outside of the application's current address space. This allows you to break large or complex programming problems into routines that can be executed independently of one another to take advantage of multiple computers. Thus, RPC makes it possible to attack a problem using a form of parallel or multi-processing.

Written from a programmer's perspective, this book shows what you can do with RPC and presents a framework for learning it.

494 pages, ISBN 0-937175-77-3

Practical C Programming

By Steve Oualline

There are lots of introductory C books, but this is the first one that has the no-nonsense, practical approach that has made Nutshell Handbooks famous. C programming is more than just getting the syntax right. Style and debugging also play a tremendous part in creating well-running programs.

Practical C Programming teaches you how to create programs that are easy to read, maintain and debug. Practical rules are stressed. For example, there are 15 precedence rules in C (&& comes before || comes before ?:). The practical programmer simplifies these down to two: 1) Multiply and divide come before addition and subtraction and 2) Put parentheses around everything else. Electronic Archaeology, the art of going through someone else's code, is also described.

Topics covered include:

- Good programming style
- C syntax: what to use and what not to use
- The programming environment, including *make*
- The total programming process
- Floating point limitations
- Tricks and surprises

Covers Turbo C (DOS) as well as the UNIX C compiler.

420 pages, ISBN 0-937175-65-X

Using C on the UNIX System

By Dave Curry

Using C on the UNIX System provides a thorough introduction to the UNIX system call libraries. It is aimed at programmers who already know C but who want to take full advantage of the UNIX programming environment. If you want to learn how to work with the operating system and if you want to write programs that can interact with directories, terminals and networks at the lowest level, you will find this book essential. It is impossible to write UNIX utilities of any sophistication without understanding the material in this book.

250 pages, ISBN 0-937175-23-4

Managing Projects with make

2nd Edition
By Steve Talbott and Andrew Oram

Make is one of UNIX's greatest contributions to software development, and this book is the clearest description of *make* ever written. Even the smallest software project typically involves a number of files that depend upon each other in various ways. If you modify one or more source files, you must relink the program after recompiling some, but not necessarily all, of the sources.

Make greatly simplifies this process. By recording the relationships between sets of files, *make* can automatically perform all the necessary updating. The 2nd Edition of this book describes all the basic features of *make* and provides guidelines on meeting the needs of large, modern projects.

152 pages, ISBN 0-937175-90-0

Checking C Programs with lint

By Ian F. Darwin

The *lint* program checker has proven itself time and again to be one of the best tools for finding portability problems and certain types of coding errors in C programs. *lint* verifies a program or program segments against standard libraries, checks the code for common portability errors, and tests the programming against some tried and true guidelines. *lint*ing your code is a necessary (though not sufficient) step in writing clean, portable, effective programs. This book introduces you to *lint*, guides you through running it on your programs and helps you to interpret *lint*'s output.

84 pages, ISBN 0-937175-30-7

DNS and BIND

By Cricket Liu and Paul Albitz

DNS and BIND is a complete guide to the Internet's Domain Name System (DNS) and the Berkeley Internet Name Domain (BIND) software, which is the UNIX implementation of DNS. DNS is the system that translates hostnames (like "rock.ora.com") into Internet addresses (like 192.54.67.23) Until BIND was developed, name translation was based on a "host table"; if you were on the Internet, you got a table that listed all the systems connected to the network, and their address. As the Internet grew from hundreds to thousands and hundreds of thousands of systems, host tables became unworkable. DNS is a distributed database that solves the same problem effectively, allowing the network to grow without constraints. Rather than having a central table that gets distributed to every system on the net, it allows local administrators to assign their own hostnames and addresses, and install these names in a local database.

418 pages, ISBN 1-56592-010-4

sed & awk

By Dale Dougherty

For people who create and modify text files, *sed* and *awk* are power tools for editing. Most of the things that you can do with these programs can be done interactively with a text editor. However, using *sed* and *awk* can save many hours of repetitive work in achieving the same result.

This book contains a comprehensive treatment of *sed* and *awk* syntax. Plus, it emphasizes the kinds of practical problems that *sed* and *awk* can help users to solve, with many useful example scripts and programs.

"*sed & awk* is a must for UNIX system programmers and administrators, and even general UNIX readers will benefit. I have over a hundred UNIX and C books in my personal library at home, but only a dozen are duplicated on the shelf where I work. This one just became number twelve."—Root Journal

414 pages, ISBN 0-937175-59-5

Programming Perl

By Larry Wall & Randal Schwartz

This is the authoritative guide to the hottest new UNIX utility in years, co-authored by the creator of that utility.

Perl is a language for easily manipulating text, files and processes. Perl provides a more concise and readable way to do many jobs that were formerly accomplished (with difficulty) by programming in the C language or one of the shells. Even though Perl is not yet a standard part of UNIX, it is likely to be available wherever you choose to work. And if it isn't, you can get it and install it easily and free of charge.

482 pages, ISBN 0-937175-64-1

UNIX for FORTRAN Programmers

By Mike Loukides

UNIX for FORTRAN Programmers provides the serious scientific programmer with an introduction to the UNIX operating system and its tools. The intent of the book is to minimize the UNIX entry barrier: to familiarize readers with the most important tools so they can be productive as quickly as possible. *UNIX for FORTRAN Programmers* shows readers how to do things that they're interested in: not just how to use a tool like *make* or *rcs*, but how it is used in program development and fits into the toolset as a whole.

"An excellent book describing the features of the UNIX FORTRAN compiler f77 and related software. This book is extremely well written."
—American Mathematical Monthly

264 pages, ISBN 0-937175-51-X